T0158058

LESSONS LEARNED IN STRANGE PLACES

JANE COOPER

Inspiring Voices®
A Service of **Guideposts**

Inspiring Voices books may be ordered through booksellers or by contacting:

Inspiring Voices
1663 Liberty Drive
Bloomington, IN 47403
www.inspiringvoices.com
1 (866) 697-5313

ISBN: 978-1-4624-0980-8 (sc)
ISBN: 978-1-4624-0981-5 (e)

Library of Congress Control Number: 2014909237

Printed in the United States of America.

Inspiring Voices rev. date: 06/19/2014

CHAPTER 1

WE DIDN'T NEED ALADDIN'S LAMP

The man rose and leaned over his desk, saying angrily to me, "I can't give you a visa for my country."

I retorted just as angrily, "Is yours the only country in the world that doesn't allow visitors?"

Sitting in the office of the Iraqi consul general, which was located in Bonn, Germany, my mother and I had no idea that it would be so difficult to get into this ancient land. As my mom said later in one of her letters to my dad, "It is easier for a rich man to enter heaven than for a Christian to enter Iraq." After all, we had no trouble earlier getting a visa for Iran, as this was 1974, when the shah was still in power.

Being a teacher for the Department of Defense Dependent Schools in Germany, I had traveled to many different countries, so when I read in our school's daily bulletin about a trip to Iraq and Iran, I was interested.

When the tour was later canceled (tours and tourists were not allowed to go to Iraq, although I didn't know that at the time), my mom and I decided to go on our own. Consequently, my mom flew over from Kansas to Germany to join me for my Christmas vacation. Just before school let out for the holidays, we had many important details to attend to with regard to our getting into Iraq, such as getting a statement from a chaplain saying we were Christians and obtaining a letter from the provost marshal stating we had no criminal records.

Getting a letter for each of us from the base chaplain was easy enough, but the provost marshal said that he could not give my mom a letter stating she had no criminal record since she neither lived nor worked on the base. Because my mom had no way of proving she was an upstanding, reputable person, we decided to try to get the visa without this piece of information.

Another important job was that of getting airline tickets. After having our schedules changed several times, we finally settled on a flight that went to Baghdad via Beirut, Lebanon, on a Middle East Airlines airplane.

Thus armed with our important letters and our airplane tickets, we headed up the Autobahn to Bonn to obtain our visas. And this is where we encountered the not-so-civil man in the Iraqi Embassy. After being told that we should have consulted him before we even got our airline tickets, this surly man finally had us wait in another room while he conferred with some other person. While waiting, my mom remarked, "If it's God's will that we take this trip, everything will work out. But if it isn't God's will, then we don't want it."

We were greatly relieved when the Iraqi man returned saying we could get our visas. There was a caveat, though—we were told we had to make reservations for a hotel in Baghdad before we left. We nodded our assent and went on our way rejoicing.

On the way back home, I noticed a peculiar odor coming from my car. Nevertheless, we went racing down the Autobahn, anxious to get home and start packing for our trip.

Since we were nearly out of food in my apartment, I decided to go to the shopette on base to buy some necessary provisions before heading home. As I pulled up to the curb, however, I found I had no brakes. Evidently this was the reason for the peculiar odor I had earlier noticed. Knowing that the auto repair shops would be closed for the next several days due to Christmas, I now had to find another way to get to the airport at Frankfurt. Fortunately, my American neighbor was willing to take us to the train station, and by train we could then reach the airport.

That night while listening to the news on the radio, we heard that the Palestine guerillas in Lebanon had been bombing Israel. Fearing that Israel might retaliate, we had extreme reservations about flying on an Arab plane. However, in the morning as we were having our devotions, I just happened to open my Bible to Psalm 118:17, which says, "I shall not die, but live." We felt then that God was telling us we would be okay. Even though we experienced so many problems already, we knew that God was in this trip and working everything out for us.

So finally, on Christmas Day, we boarded the MEA plane and were on our way, but our problems were far from over. When we landed in Beirut, I made a big mistake. Instead of going to the waiting area where we could board our plane for Baghdad, I inadvertently got a transit visa for Lebanon. Consequently, we were now headed for Beirut rather than Baghdad. Fortunately, I was able to find someone in the airport who spoke English and who could help us get to the right area. Getting there, however, necessitated our going clear outside onto the tarmac. As we walked outside, we noticed soldiers with machine guns standing in strategic places, which gave us a rather disconcerted feeling.

It was with much relief when we finally got to the right area. And what a kaleidoscope of costumes we saw in this waiting room—women in their burkas and sheikhs with their long robes and unusual headdresses. It was almost like Halloween. My mom and I sat there wide-eyed as we watched and heard various airline personnel calling out the flights to places like Kuwait, Amman, Riyadh, and so on. Evidently, many of the people could not read the boards telling of the various flights.

Finally it was our time to board the plane. At around midnight we landed at the Baghdad airport. I've never before or since seen an airport quite as primitive as this one. After getting off the plane, we entered a room with long board tables onto which they put our luggage. As soon as we retrieved our luggage, we then held up our passports to a single man at the door, and it seemed if we smiled prettily enough, he would let us go on through.

Once we got into the outer waiting area of the tiny airport, we soon realized that because of the late hour, few people were working. And most of the people from our plane had already hopped into taxis and were on their way home. When I did spot one of the few available taxis, I found the driver could speak no English. What a predicament we were in now! We had no way to get to Baghdad, and once we got there we had no hotel! Even though we had promised the official at the Iraqi Embassy we would get a hotel before leaving Germany, and we had indeed tried, we never did get a reservation.

I said to my mom as she stood outside where the taxis were parked, "Pray that we find a way into Baghdad or that someone comes along to help us." I then went back inside. About that time a woman came up to me (an American, I thought, as she spoke American English) and asked me, "Are you with the oil companies?" to which I replied, "No, we are tourists."

"Tourists!" she almost shouted. "How did you ever get a visa for Iraq?" Then calming down a bit, she asked if I needed any help.

I replied with great relief, "Yes, we need to get a taxi for Baghdad."

Leaving me for a short time, she soon returned, this time telling me that she and her husband would take us into Baghdad in their van. They had come to the airport to pick up friends who were visiting them from Germany for the Christmas holidays (evidently a person could get a visa if he or she was visiting friends in Iraq), and they had enough room for two more people in their van.

On the way into town, a drive of about ten miles, we found out a little about this couple. Jim, the husband, was a German who taught the children of people connected to the German Embassy. (At this time there was no American Embassy in Iraq.) His wife, Sue, was an American who was a member of the Church of the Brethren, the church college from which my mom and I had both graduated. It turned out to be a small world indeed!

As we drove along, Sue suggested that my mom and I would we better off if we stayed with them in their home while in Baghdad. When planning out this trip neither one of us had realized how difficult it would be not only to get into this country, but also how dangerous it was once there, as Iraq at this time was a police state with secret police everywhere.

In fact, just a few days before arriving in Baghdad, the city officials had hung six Jewish people in a downtown square known as the "Hanging Square." And when we were at the airport leaving to fly on to Iran, we met a woman from South America who was making an around-the-world trip. She told us that because she had no visa for Iraq, she was not allowed to leave the airport; and when she even went into the restroom, someone followed her. So for Mom and me to stay with people who knew their way around and who were trustworthy seemed like the perfect plan.

In addition to us two Americans and the two German friends they had picked up at the airport, this couple also had staying in their home a young Swedish woman who was smuggling parts of the Bible up to northern Iraq to the Kurdish people, and her Swedish boyfriend, plus an Iraqi couple. This was quite a united nations!

We appreciated the hospitality of Sue and her husband, not only for giving us a bed in which to sleep, but also for providing meals. There was one problem, though. The Arab man, when being passed a bowl of rice for dinner one evening, ate directly from the bowl instead of putting the rice on his plate. From that time on, my mom, who was somewhat of a health nut, would not eat any more rice!

In defense of Mom, though, Mae, the Swedish woman, told of a time she was invited into a Kurdish home for lunch, where they served, in addition to rice, a salad of green lettuce. She said she thought the lettuce was covered with dirt, but then noticed that all the dirt was moving!

On our first day in Bagdad, Jim, our host, took us around the city and even out to the ruins of the ancient city of Babylon, where we saw nothing much but fragments of blue tiles scattered around. In Bagdad we visited the bazaar, where I checked out the jewelry in the various small booths. The jewelry was mostly made of gold and was very beautiful, but because it was sold by weight at the current price of gold, it was also very expensive.

The bazaar was quite unique, being divided into sections according to what was being sold. For instance, one street would be sheep products (wool and skins); another was the aluminum area, where the vendors sat and pounded designs in the pots and pans they were selling; another was so unpleasant (I suppose the areas where animals were being slaughtered) that it made us sick to our stomachs.

As we drove around the city of Bagdad, we noticed men on the sidewalks with a little outdoors-type oven in which they were baking a small round loaf of bread that had big bubbles in it. A type of brush called "camel" or "fire" brush grew out on the flat plains, and the people gathered these to burn in their ovens. Once we saw a whole pile of brush walking along, and a second later we noticed a woman under it! We also saw people along the streets warming themselves over these little stoves or ovens, or sometimes they were just using pans of coal. They evidently had no heat in their homes.

Since my mom was interested in seeing where the old city of Nineveh had been located (the city there now is called Mosul), we headed out the following day on our own along with the two German guests. Not being able to get reservations on either a train or a plane, we took a bus as far as the city of Kirkuk, from where we would then take a taxi on up to Mosul. (Taxis were reasonable since gas was only twenty-five cents a gallon.)

However, we never would have gotten a taxi had it not been for a kindly Iraqi man, for many taxi drivers, when finding out our nationality, would say, "No Americans!" This man had ridden the bus up to Kirkuk with us and called a taxi for us once we got to the bus station. He also bought some orange pop for us to drink while waiting and even invited us to visit him at his home!

As we headed out in the taxi for Mosul, we passed a car on a bridge which had struck a woman standing at the end of the bridge. Our taxi stopped and then went on, so we never knew if the woman was badly hurt or not. We found many of the people in this country to be very poor drivers. In fact, one visitor said to Mom, "One had better have their life insurance up to date to even cross the streets!"

It took around nine hours to travel up to Mosul, and was, therefore, late when we arrived. Finding a hotel in connection with the train station, we rented rooms for two nights. My mom was quite surprised to discover the words, "Iraqi Government Hotel" sewn in Arabic on the bedspreads in our room, which looked just like the English number "666."

The next day we went to see the remains of the ancient city of Nineveh, which consisted of a single piece of foundation down in the ground. We then spent the rest of the day wandering around Mosul, which we found to be one of the dirtiest cities we'd ever been in. Water from the sewers seemed to be running from the houses out across the sidewalks into the streets.

As we were preparing to leave in the morning, we found that the highway we were going to take back to Baghdad was closed due to the Kurds fighting in that area, and so we had to take a different route back. Once back in the home of Jim and Sue, we spent our last evening sitting around in the kitchen singing religious choruses. After we had sung for a while, the Arab visitor pulled out a song from under his robe and began singing to us. But neither my mom nor I appreciated his music, nor any of the other Iraqi music, which we had been hearing everywhere we went.

After packing our suitcases the next morning, we headed once again for the airport. We flew on an Iraqi plane, a new cream and green-striped Boeing 737. We had a smooth flight en route to Iran and were very happy to be leaving Iraq, as we had had a claustrophobic feeling all the time we were there, even though Sue had kept telling us we were one in five hundred people who ever got to go to Iraq.

When we arrived at the airport in Tehran, we found that part of the airport roof had collapsed due to a heavy snowfall. But even so, we were able to retrieve our luggage and book a room in a supposedly deluxe hotel—The Park.

Spending the night on hard beds in a cold room, we got up the next morning and walked around the downtown area of Tehran, even finding several souvenirs to add to our collections: a doll for Mom and a piece of jewelry for me. We saw many beggars out on the street and even some drunks. Once we passed a man sitting by the side of the street selling hot grilled beets, and as we watched, he expectorated a hunk of spit that landed on the beets he had for sale. But as Mom said, "What's a little spit added to your food anyway!"

Neither one of us particularly enjoyed the food we got in either Iraq or Iran. It usually consisted of rice and more rice, sometimes boiled with beans and sometimes with lamb or goat meat. Once I ordered something that was supposed to be poultry, but what I got was about ten little meat pieces that looked like very tiny drumsticks. We didn't know what it was, but it really didn't taste too bad.

In the afternoon of our first day there, we took a bus tour to several places, including the big bank vault—their Fort Knox— where all their crown jewels were kept. There we saw huge pans and buckets full and practically running over with diamonds, rubies, emeralds, and sapphires, besides all the crowns, robes, thrones, and jewelry set with them. In there, too, is the famous Peacock Throne, which is covered with gold and set with jewels. One of their shahs stole it back in the 1700s from India. My mom wondered why they didn't sell some of these jewels and help the beggars and poor out on the street.

Since my mom had a bad cold (no doubt having been picked up in Iraq because of the coldness of Jim's and Sue's home), she spent the next day resting in bed in our hotel room. Because it was New Year's Day, not many stores were open, but I did find a pharmacy open, where I bought Mom some chewable vitamin C. There was one problem, though—they made her foam at the mouth every time she ate one.

I walked quite a distance that day down to the bazaar, but only found a shop or two open. The traffic in this city was crazy.

Cars seemed to go in all directions on a single street. And once I saw a man with a flock of turkeys crossing the street in the midst of all the traffic!

Feeling a bit better the next day, my mom decided we could travel down to the city of Isfahan, a city some 250 miles south of Tehran, noted for its many beautiful mosques. However, we were unable to get reservations on a plane, so settled on taking a bus instead. We went by taxi to the bus station, where I was able to purchase two one-way tickets. As we sat and waited for our bus to leave, I figured out the Iranian number system and, thus, knew what seats we were assigned. We also watched the various people at the water fountain getting a drink from a single plastic cup that was sitting on the edge of the fountain.

Once aboard the bus, we realized that, other than a German couple, we were the only foreigners on the bus. It was an eight-hour ride through mountainous areas on narrow winding roads to Isfahan.

The bus stopped three times to let people use toilets in small villages along the way. I got off once and found the accommodations to be very primitive—just a hole in the ground with a single dim light hanging above and a small wooden door that gave some privacy. Once back on the bus, I watched as a boy steward came around every so often with a big plastic pitcher of water and gave people a drink. Fortunately, he had paper cups, so people didn't all have to drink from the same cup.

Once one of the ladies on the bus, evidently feeling sorry for Mom and me since we had had nothing to eat on that long ride, pulled a sack of candy out from under her long black burka and offered us each a piece. We noticed that the ladies had all sorts of things under their robes. One lady even pulled a baby out toward the end of the journey. We wondered what else they may have hidden under their burkas.

When we reached Isfahan it was dark, and an Iranian Air Force man helped us get a taxi to the Shah Abass Hotel, a deluxe hotel that had been converted from an old camel caravan stopover place. We found tourists staying in this hotel from many different countries.

After a good night's rest, we decided that the first thing we should do before any sightseeing was to get plane tickets back to Tehran. But at the airline terminal we found that no seats were available. There was nothing else to do—we would have to once again take the bus back. However, when I went to the depot of the bus line we had taken down, they had no seats available either. We were frantic—here we were 250 miles from Tehran and due to fly back to Germany the next morning. I finally left Mom sitting in the depot, praying, while I rushed from one depot to another looking for some other bus we could ride. Finally locating one we could take back, I discovered it wouldn't be leaving until three in the afternoon, which meant we would get into Tehran around midnight.

Having spent such a long time getting a bus, we didn't have much time left to look around Isfahan. However, we did walk down to the square, where I found a vendor selling copper items and was able to buy several pieces. We also viewed one of the many large mosques while at the village square.

Getting back to the bus depot, we located our seats on the bus and settled down for the long ride back. Before the bus pulled out, the driver led all the Moslems in a prayer (for safety, we assumed). On the way it started raining on us as we were going through the mountains. The people were tense with fear, as the roads were narrow, winding, and slick. Once along the way we came upon a terrible accident— a bus turned over on its side in the middle of the highway. We wondered if it could have been one of the buses we were unable to get on.

When we finally made it safely through the mountains, the driver and the people said another prayer (maybe of thanksgiving). But we weren't out of danger yet, as a dense fog descended on us, and the driver could not see a thing. He just crept along with his head stuck out of the window. But after the long, fearful drive, we at last reached Tehran. It was pouring rain as we stood and waited for a taxi to take us to our hotel. Once back in our room, we repacked our luggage, had room service bring us a sandwich, as we hadn't had anything to eat since breakfast, and asked the front desk for a 4:00 a.m. wake-up call.

Hurrying by taxi to the airport early in the morning, we boarded a Pan Am flight, enjoying the small breakfast we were served as we headed for Ankara, Turkey. I especially appreciated the American coffee, as I had found the thick, dark, bitter coffee we'd been drinking to be quite distasteful.

Thinking all of our problems were over once we reached the airline terminal in Ankara, we were dismayed when we found our tickets were not confirmed on the Ankara to Istanbul segment of our journey. Again leaving my mom to pray about the situation, I went from one airline to another to see if we could get on another flight out of Ankara, but to no avail. We had been put on a waiting list and were seventh on the list, so the situation seemed hopeless. Soon our flight aboard the Turkish plane was called, and my mom and I simply walked out and boarded the plane. Since there were no assigned seats, we just sat down where we found two seats together. And we were off!

The plane we were flying to Istanbul was a Turkish plane, but we discovered when the tray table fell in my mom's lap that the plane was in actuality an old Pan Am plane (as the tray table indicated) that had been repainted with the Turkish name and symbols. We found nothing on the plane seemed to be working properly—not the seat belts, nor the shades, and, as mentioned, the tray table. We wondered if the engines would work! However, we made it safely to Istanbul, where we then boarded a German Lufthansa plane going to Frankfurt. As we touched down in Germany, we realized what a harrowing but extremely eventful trip we had had. We certainly hadn't needed a magic lantern, since all along the route God had taken care of us by meeting all our needs.

LESSON NO. 1

THE IMPORTANCE OF DOING GOD'S WILL

When my mom said, "If it's God's will it will work out, and if it isn't His will, then we don't want it" (i.e., our trip to Iraq and Iran), I never realized how this statement would impact me; for I have now inculcated this idea to be the philosophy of my life.

The most important decision we can ever make is the decision to serve God. When we give ourselves completely to Him and then determine to follow His rules, we can then know His will. And His will is always the best for us. In fact, I don't believe God ever has second-bests for His kids. But sometimes His will means waiting—maybe even quite awhile. And this is where people may get into trouble, for waiting can be discouraging at times. However, if we do our own thing, we can ruin the wonderful plans God will eventually work out for us.

Doing God's will, then, is very important. For what it means, in reality, is keeping God's commandments and doing what He tells us to do. And by keeping His commandments, we show the world that we are His children.

Sometimes as children of God, though, we do our own thing instead of His will. We call this sinning, and when we go our own way and do our own thing, our relationship to God is broken. Therefore, whenever we sin, we need to repent immediately, for there is no such thing as a sinful Christian. This is an oxymoron. It's similar to calling a shrimp a giant. But we know that once we repent, God forgives, and we're back on the right track.

LESSON NO. 2

A VERSE IN TIME OF NEED

The Word of God, or the Bible, is not just static words on a sheet of paper; His Word is alive. In other words, when we read verses in the Bible, it is as though God, Himself, is speaking directly to us. And when we have a problem, a need, or a question, we can find help by seeking for the answer in His Word.

I have, at various times, asked God to give me a special verse for a specific problem and have opened up the Bible and found just the answer I needed. For instance, once when I was flying back to my job overseas, I missed my original flight, which then necessitated my taking another airline. As I sat in my seat before takeoff, I became extremely fearful, even to the point of thinking that this plane was going to crash. So I pulled out of my purse a little New Testament, which included the book of Psalms, and I asked God to give me a verse that would calm my fears. Opening up the little New Testament, I glanced down at a verse on the page before me that stated, "Hold thou me up and I shall be safe" (Psalm 119:117). This was just the antidote I needed, for I could then picture God holding His Hands under the plane, and I no longer had any fear.

Is it wrong to ask God for a particular verse? And the answer is an emphatic no! God always knows our needs, and He has just the right answer for us in His Word. So that morning before our Middle East trip when I opened up to the verse, "I shall not die, but live," I knew this was an answer from God telling us He would take care of us. And even though we had many problems along the way, God worked out each problem in His own way and time.

CHAPTER 2

PINECONES AND MOSQUITO BITES

Since my mom is featured in so many of the stories in this book, I thought it only appropriate to tell a little about her.

Having three main interests in life—nature, travel, and God—my mom pursued these interests to the diversion of other things: housework, for instance. She would far rather spend an evening outdoors studying the stars than to clean house or do dishes. It's not that she was dirty, but some things in life took priority to housework. My mom was very exact when it came to business matters, but she tended to become aggravated with me when I even tried to straighten up her lingerie drawer by putting her underwear in neat little piles. She'd rather have everything in one mixed-up mess!

But nature, now that was an entirely different matter. One time when my mom and I were driving around California, she had me stop when she spotted a large stand of pine trees. Having heard about pinecones that were as large as a child's head, she thought if she walked back in the woods, she just might find some of these particular cones. After having been gone for what seemed like hours, all-of-a-sudden, up over a small rise my mom appeared, her arms filled with large pinecones. And these particular cones were not easy to carry. Called "digger pinecones," they had sharp-pointed scales turned up at the ends, which tore at one's skin every time they were picked up. My mom had fallen once and had torn her skirt, slip, and panties, but she had held tightly onto the cones and had not lost a single one.

Another bad experience for Mom occurred in Florida. On a trip one summer through the South, she was looking forward to seeing a particular constellation called "The Southern Cross." So when we got down to a lake in Central Florida, we went out after dark certain we would see that constellation. We scanned the sky but never did glimpse anything that looked like a cross. However, the next morning, to my mom's consternation, her legs and arms were covered with itchy red spots. She had been so busy scanning the sky she never realized that dozens of mosquitoes were attacking her!

Going back to college later in life, Mom decided to take a course in entomology. One requirement for the course was to make a collection of various insects—dead, of course—to be displayed neatly in boxes. At first she went outdoors with a butterfly net and tried capturing as many bugs and butterflies as possible. Eventually the neighborhood kids, when finding out what she was doing, decided to get in on the action. Several times I went to the door only to have some kid reach out his hand to me, saying, "Here's some bugs for ya."

Mom finally decided that her bugs and butterflies would be in a better condition if she raised them herself. Knowing what the worms of monarch butterflies looked like, Mom started collecting as many as she could find. She then brought the worms into the house and put them in jars, together with the plants they ate. Eventually each worm turned into a chrysalis and then into a butterfly. It was exciting to watch a butterfly, fresh out of its cocoon, pump color into its wings and then fly away. There were a few problems in connection with this raising of butterflies, though. One night when my mom was turning back the covers of her bed, getting ready to hop in and go to sleep, I heard a loud scream. It seems one of the worms had gotten out of its jar and had found her bed!

There were other odd places I also found signs of nature. Once when opening the refrigerator, I spotted a plastic bag with a tiny bird in it. My mom had found a dead bird lying in the street that she didn't recognize. So picking it up, she brought it home, leaving it in the refrigerator until she had time to identify it.

Another love of Mom's was flowers. It didn't matter what kind—wild or domesticated—she was interested in them all. Spotting some wildflowers growing by the side of the highway on a trip we took through the West one summer, she insisted I stop so she could dig up the plants, intending to take them all the way back to Kansas. Before we got home, though, those raggedy plants had been in eight different states. We had even carried them into and out of California, and this was at the time that California had border controls that checked all produce and plant life brought into the state.

For several years I taught school in western Kansas. In the hills south of the town of Oakley were some of the best fossil beds found anywhere in the United States. One Saturday when my mom had come out to visit me, we had a very profitable day searching in these hills and finding both a fossil bird's tooth and a fossil shark's tooth.

But on another visit to this location, an area twenty miles from the nearest town and having no farm homes nearby, we ran into trouble. It had rained the night before, and the roads, being dirt, had turned into mud. Unfortunately, my car got stuck in the mud clear up to the tops of the hubcaps. I was getting quite concerned, knowing we could be stuck for days before anyone found us. So we did what we always knew worked: we prayed. It wasn't long until a man in a truck appeared who just "happened" to have a chain. Attaching the chain to my car, the man pulled us out of our predicament in a short time.

Besides loving nature, my mom also loved to travel. One summer when I had come home from Europe, where I had been teaching, my folks and I made plans to attend a "Full Gospel Business Men's Fellowship" meeting in Dallas, Texas. I had gotten up on the morning we were to leave and had prepared breakfast, had done up the dishes, packed both my dad's and my suitcases, and had gotten the car ready. During all that time my mom had been packing her suitcase. But when we stopped for the night at Gainesville, Texas, my mom discovered that even though she had spent all morning getting her suitcase ready, she had not packed any pajamas!

Being very health conscious, Mom would always spray the entire bathroom with Lysol at every motel room in which we stayed. (She would also spray me and everything I touched when I had a cold or the flu.) She had, however, no control over the restaurants where we ate.

Staying in a hotel in Honolulu, we had been eating breakfast in the hotel restaurant until one morning when I picked up my napkin from off the table and a cockroach ran out from under it. We also had enjoyed having macadamia nut pancakes for breakfast. Since the cockroach incident, however, we had no more macadamia nut pancakes. It tended to remind my mom of the time in Texas when she had been eating a donut and discovered half a cockroach in the piece that was left.

My dad was not much of a traveler and was always content to "mind the fires" at home while we took off on our own. We found, however, that there were times when having my dad with us would have made us feel much safer. One night while traveling in Montana, heading to the city of Roundup, we began to feel frightened as we drove down the highway at midnight. We almost began to feel this might be our "last roundup!"

We also would have felt better about repairs to our car had my dad been along. On our trip to the West, we were told in Nevada that unless we had the wheels of our car packed, we wouldn't make it all the way back home. Fortunately, we did make it home, and we later found out that some filling stations in Nevada made it a practice of giving people bad advice about their cars.

My mom's third interest, and actually her main interest, was that of working for and serving God. Because my dad was a minister, my mom would occasionally preach. She had only one sermon, though—one on hell. One Sunday evening she was going to give her hell sermon to my dad's congregation. She had been praying that the Easter/Christmas-only attendees would actually come to an ordinary Sunday evening service. But as she studied and prayed, rain began to fall, and so she began praying that the rain would stop. However, God soon spoke to her and told her that He could bring the people out even in the rain. And sure enough, when she went over to the church, there they sat—the people she had been praying would come out on a Sunday evening in the rain!

In one church in which my dad pastored, there was a family who became good friends with my folks. Consequently, my mom became hopeful that the mother in the family would give her heart and life to the Lord—would get "born again," in other words. One weekday afternoon my mom decided to drive out into the country to have a talk with this lady. It had rained the night before, and Mom, not knowing that the local people never used one particular road after a rain, headed down this very road. She hadn't gone very far when the car turned completely around in the mud and headed back toward town. This happened several times, and once the car even slid down into the ditch. However, after much effort and much prayer, my mom finally made it to a better road. Having but a short time to speak to her friend about the Lord before her girls arrived home from school, Mom hurriedly explained the way of salvation and led her to the Lord.

Always concerned about people, my mom learned an important lesson one Christmas. Busy decorating the church for a Christmas Eve service, Mom was startled when a man appeared in the doorway, blocking the only entrance into and out of the church. When Mom asked him what he wanted, he replied that he needed to find some work to earn money for food. Since it was starting to grow dark outside, Mom's only thought was to get the man out of the church. So she sent the stranger out to see my dad, who was at that time doing some carpentry work on a parishioner's home. Later, when my dad came home to eat supper, Mom noticed that the man was not with him. After telling Mom he knew of no work for the man, my dad, along with Mom, grew concerned knowing that they could have at least given the stranger something to eat. Consequently, they got in the car and searched the entire small town where we lived, never finding him. But from that time on, my mom made sure she always took in anyone who came to the parsonage needing something to eat.

My folks, when they could, attended other church services so they could be in a better position of advising people about various beliefs that other congregations held. They also attended as many services of well-known evangelists as possible.

One Saturday, at Mom's suggestion, we drove from Kansas down to Oklahoma City to hear Billy Graham speak. Planning on returning home that same day, we noticed it was getting late when we got back up into Kansas.

Once in the dark, my dad got lost. Pulling up beside a car that was stopped at a stop sign, Dad asked for the directions we needed to go. However, he soon realized that the men he was questioning were drunk. And so we pulled quickly out onto the highway and headed out, not really knowing just where we were headed.

We no sooner had gotten onto the highway when we became aware that the other car was following us. My dad speeded up, and they did too. Thus, here we were racing down a highway around midnight not knowing where we were or where we were going being chased by two drunks. Soon, however, we saw a sign that said, "Welcome to Harper County," a county that was in the opposite direction we wanted to go. In the meantime, the headlights of the other car had disappeared. As we turned around and headed back in the direction from which we had come, we saw the men who had been chasing us beside the highway trying to thumb a ride, their car down in the ditch. We knew then that God was really watching over us.

LESSON NO. 3

IMPORTANT LESSONS ON TRAVELING AND LIVING TOGETHER

One lesson I learned about traveling or living with another person is the importance of being unselfish. A selfish person does not make either a good mate or a good traveling partner. For instance, when my mom wanted me to stop the car so she could dig up flowers by the side of the road, had I said, "No, we don't have time," and had gone on down the highway, things later that day would not have worked out for our best. We might not have found a good motel or a good place to eat, or we might have even lost something along the way. Or, if when I said to my mom, "I need to stop driving and find a place to stay for the night," she had replied, "No, we need to go on a ways yet," again nothing would work out quite right for us.

A second lesson of traveling or living with someone is the importance of getting along. The Bible says, "Can two walk together except they be agreed?" (Amos 3:3). And 1 Peter 3:7 says, when speaking of marriage: "You husbands likewise, live with your wives in an understanding way, as with a weaker vessel, since she is a woman; and grant her honor as a fellow of heir of the grace of life so that your prayers may not be hindered."

It's important to note that when two people living or traveling together don't get along or have discords, even their prayers will be unanswered. Sometimes people may wonder why God is not answering their prayers, and the reason may be because of arguments, disagreements, or unkindness to another person.

A third lesson in living or traveling together is the importance of controlling the mouth. Contrary to the old adage, "Sticks and stones may break my bones, but words can never hurt me," words many times do more damage than being hit by stones. The reason for this is that words may never be forgotten, and people, especially children, tend to become what they're told they are. So if a person is told he is no good, he may begin to believe that. Therefore, it's important to weigh one's words before saying them aloud. And anything that can harm should never be spoken.

The Bible says in Ecclesiastes 10:12, "Words from the mouth of a wise man are gracious, while the lips of a fool consume him." In other words, a righteous person will speak words that are helpful, inspirational, and kind, while the unrighteous speak nonsense and unkindness. It's better to bite one's tongue and not say what's on the tip of the tongue than to ruin another person's life.

Jesus even told his disciples that we'll give an account for every idle word that we speak, and that by our words we'll either be justified or condemned (Matthew 12:36–37) Therefore, we should determine to be like David when he said, "I am purposed that my mouth shall not transgress" (Psalm 17:36).

A fourth very important lesson that everyone needs to learn, but especially people living, working, or traveling together, is that of forgiveness. We all make mistakes and occasionally do wrong. As the old proverb says, "To err is human, but to forgive is divine," Therefore, it's important to quickly forgive the one who hurt you and to never hold a grudge. For grudge-holding does more damage to those who contain these two faults than these faults do to the person who actually did the wrong. In fact, forgiveness is one of the greatest gifts one person can give to another, for it is the greatest gift God gives to us.

CHAPTER 3

BEHIND THE IRON CURTAIN

Teaching on a small military base in Amberg, Germany, I shared an upstairs apartment with three other teachers who also taught at the same American school. A spur-of-the-moment decision by one of my roommates once to celebrate a birthday in Pilsen, Czechoslovakia, a distance of some fifty miles from Amberg, meant leaving right after our school day was over.

When we arrived in Pilsen, we found a restaurant where we enjoyed a typical meal. After we had finished our meal, a waiter then brought out a large cake that Bev, the gal with the car and the idea, had bought at a German Konditerei (bakery) before leaving Amberg. We had earlier asked the waiter to bring out the cake at the close of our meal with the candles, which we had brought with us, on the cake. Evidently he didn't understand the custom of blowing out candles on cakes, and when the cake arrived at our table, the candles were all lying around the sides of the cake!

We left Pilsen late that night, and when we arrived at the border, all the lights at the small border station were put out so a guard could shine a bright light on each person's face. After checking our faces with our passports, we then had to get out of the car so the guard could remove the backseat, checking to make sure no person was underneath. When the truck and the underneath part of the car had been inspected, we were then free to cross over into Germany. Such was my first experience of entering and leaving a Communist country!

A few years later, while I was teaching in Nürnberg, Germany, in the 1970s, my mom had the American Bible Society send me some Bibles in the Polish and Czech languages. Bibles were strictly forbidden in Communist countries, as I found out once on a trip to Romania. As we approached the border, I noticed a large sign that said in English, "No Bibles, no pornography, no comic books are allowed to be brought in." It was, then, with much trepidation that I obtained a visa for Czechoslovakia, got a train ticket to travel from Nürnberg to Prague, and packed the Bibles I was planning to smuggle in and secretly give out to people.

The train click clacked along through the rolling green hills and pleasant mountain passages of West Germany until we reach the Czech border. After we crossed over into Czechoslovakia, soldiers boarded the train. When we arrived at the first large city—Pilsen—a lady sitting in my compartment on the train said to me in German that the soldiers would be going through everyone's luggage.

I was, at this point, feeling very fearful, for I knew that even bringing in one Bible meant a lifetime sentence in prison for that person. Consequently, I began to earnestly pray that I and my Bibles would be safe. After what seemed like hours had passed by, and I had been hearing the soldiers clomping up and down the passageway of the train and heard them banging compartment doors open and shut, people started getting off the train, and in a short time we were on our way to Prague. The soldiers never did come into our compartment!

I got a slightly different taste of what a Communist country was like while taking a tour of the Balkan countries in 1983. In late afternoon we landed at the airport in Budapest, Hungary, via our "Malev Air" Russian-built plane. On the first evening we were there we boarded a tour bus to go to a restaurant and saw about a dozen other buses in the parking lot. Inside the building were long rows of tables with the entire place just packed with people. The whole experience was very touristy and unappealing.

On Easter Sunday morning, as we went out early to the bus to leave for Romania, we discovered candy in each seat of the bus. The Easter Bunny had made it safely across the border! Stopping for lunch at a small Hungarian town, we realized the people working in the restaurant had gone all out to fix us a special meal. We started our meal with goose-liver pâté, a specialty in this country for Easter. Next we had a bowl of soup. Then came the main course, consisting of pieces of liver and pork with fried onions, french fries, carrots, bing cherries, and red cabbage. For dessert we had a piece of chocolate cake filled with chocolate icing. And then to end with, we had small cups of Turkish coffee. Everything was very good but was much more than most of us could eat. One of the men on the tour said, "Let's leave before they bring us another course!" I found throughout the entire trip, however, that we were given far more food then we could eat, and, consequently, much food went to waste. This was sad, too, because the native people did not get food to eat like we were being fed. In fact, they very seldom had meat to eat.

When we reached the Romanian border later that day, we saw a large sign in English that said, "Welcome to hospitable Romania." But directly underneath the sign was a car that had all its contents lying out on a cement slab, plus everything out of the suitcases also. I thought, "How incongruous."

As we filed off the bus one at a time, so the soldiers could check us with our passport picture, my coat caught in the back door, and the door slammed shut. Since I couldn't get my coat out of the door, I filed by the soldiers without a coat and with a big wooden cross hanging around my neck! This was my introduction to Communist Romania! We were at the border three hours, and when we finally got our passports back and headed out, we had our Romanian tour guide with us.

I noticed how primitive Romania was as we drove along. We saw very few cars on the highway. Mostly we saw horse-drawn carts, which the people were using for transportation. The houses in the small villages did not seem to have indoor plumbing (this was true in all the other Balkan countries also), but had an outdoor well or pump, which was out along the street. After it got dark, we noticed very few lights on in the villages, as the people were very energy conscious. Many of the homes had a little cross on them somewhere, usually on the roof. This was to indicate where an Orthodox family lived. They put the cross on the roof so the Catholics and Moslems wouldn't bother them.

As we drove along the highway we passed a filling station where a mile long line of cars was waiting to get gas. There weren't too many filling stations in these countries and gas was rationed—hence, the long lines! I also noticed long lines of people in the capital city of Bucharest waiting to get either cheese or butter. Cheese and meat were very difficult to get. In fact, farmers could not kill their livestock without permission from the government.

Once when we stopped in a little farm village to visit a church, I skipped the church visitation and instead walked down the road to where some men were standing around talking. One of the men asked me if I was an American, and when I said yes, he told me to wait while he went to his small house. He came back shortly with a photograph of his daughter, who was from New York City and was visiting him. A little later this same man said to me, "un moment," and disappeared down into the cellar of his house, coming back with two apples for me. (I later discovered that the apples were wormy, but the thought was appreciated anyway!)

As we drove on toward Bucharest, I noticed many flocks of sheep along the side of the road. We also started seeing snow-capped mountains in the distance. In some of the villages through which we passed, I spotted storks, which had arrived back from Africa and were building their nests on the tops of some of the houses.

When we got into Bucharest, it was already dark. The people were just going home for the evening, and the streetcars were so filled that one of them was actually tilting to the side.

We took a tour of Bucharest the next day, visiting an open-air museum and, later, a Romanian school. We were allowed to go into one of the classes at the school, which was a foreign language class. They were studying English—it being the second language of Romania. When we first entered the room, the students all stood up and remained standing as long as we were there. They, of course, all wore uniforms with Young Pioneer scarves around their necks.

The next morning we left to go into Bulgaria. At the Romanian border, however, one of the teachers on our tour could not find her passport, so she had to get her suitcase off the bus and take everything out on the sidewalk to look for it. One person on the bus thought that it would make an interesting picture and snapped a photo of the girl searching for her passport just at the moment the soldier came onto the bus to look at our passports. He yelled, "No, no," at the lady, but it was already too late, so he made her take the film out of her camera. It was strictly forbidden to take pictures at the border of a Communist country. She later did get her film back, however, as our guide gave the soldier two packs of cigarettes for it. Leaving our Romanian guide at the border, we picked up a Bulgarian guide on the other side.

Bulgaria surprised me because so much of it is mountainous—about three-fourths, in fact. While taking a tour of the city of Sophia, we noticed how much the architecture looked like Stalinist Russia, since Bulgaria was very closely aligned to Russia. One of the first places we were taken to visit was a Greek Orthodox church. Our guide, being a good party member, told us that only 20 percent of the people in Bulgaria were believers, and that the young people only believed in the disco, dancing, and things of that nature. She made it sound as if only old people, and not many of them, believed in God. Of course, she had no knowledge of all the underground churches that were in these Communist countries.

In all these countries, wherever our bus stopped, men would approach us and offer to exchange money, actually for much more than the official rate. Our guides told us not to exchange money with these people, however, as it was illegal to do so, and we could get cheated. The truth of the matter was that the Communist government wanted to control the money situation, and thus we ended up getting less money for our dollar at the banks because of the lower rate. The people in these countries wanted American dollars because there were shops that had American and other foreign-made merchandise that could only be bought with American dollars.

There were several interesting things I noticed about these countries as we drove around all the large cities. One observation was that all of the street workers were women. Our guide told us that women had equal work opportunities! I also noticed that parked cars had no windshield wipers. Since car parts were so hard to get, the owners took the wipers off when the car was parked because, otherwise, they would get stolen.

After a short trip through Yugoslavia, we ended up back where we had started, in Hungary, where we boarded a German plane and flew back to Germany.

Another interesting trip made to a Communist country—this time to Yugoslavia—was when my mother came over to visit me while I was teaching on an American base in Italy. After getting a clearance to go into a Communist country (this was a requirement for all American military personnel), we headed out one December day for the capital city of Belgrade. Once over the border I was at a loss to know how to talk to the natives, as they mostly spoke a Slovakian language. We couldn't even read the signs on their stores, as most of them were either Cyrillic or Greek letters. This made it especially difficult to purchase souvenirs, get hotel rooms, and order meals. We noticed that the people on the street just stared at us. They looked glum and unhappy, and even if we smiled at them, they wouldn't smile back.

They seemed to live under very primitive conditions. In one area through which we passed, the country homes all had an outdoor well (as was earlier mentioned in the trip to Romania), where water was drawn with a rope, pulley, and bucket. And sometimes on the rims of these stone wells a washbowl and pitcher (similar to those selling in antique shops in the States) would be sitting. In some of the mountain homes we noticed that the people lived in the upper story of the house, and the animals lived down underneath—all in the same house. "A cozy arrangement," I thought. The mountain people were butchering hogs as we drove along, and they just left the gutted hogs hanging up outside in trees. I came to the conclusion that this was what the United States must have been like two centuries ago.

Staying overnight in Belgrade, we left the next day to drive back to Zagreb, the Communist headquarters of Yugoslavia. We drove only about fifty miles before running into dense fog. It was terrible—dense, freezing fog for two hundred miles—and to make matters worse, this highway running from Belgrade to Zagreb had potholes all the way. It was only a two-lane highway, also, and seemed to be paved with towering trucks that I could hardly see around or pass as they drove right down the middle of the highway with their bright lights on and with no rhyme or reason to their driving style. It was around nine at night when we finally reached Zagreb.

Finding a hotel, we went to our room and crawled into bed, collapsing with fatigue and sleepiness. On getting up the next morning, my mom had a sore throat. One problem during the night was that the bedsheets were too short, and our feet stuck out at the bottom. Also, if we inadvertently sat down on the end of the bed, the bed turned up on one end, and we fell off onto the floor. When we went down to breakfast in the morning, we carried our tote bags with us but were accosted by the waiter, who told us we could not take our tote bags into the breakfast room but would have to check them. Since we were leaving that morning anyway, we just took them out to the car instead. When we came back he now said that we could not take our coats into the breakfast room as well but would have to check them too. (We had eaten in some of the finest restaurants all over Europe along with our tote bags and coats with no problems ever. But this was Communism.) Mom told the waiter she was cold, but he kept insisting that the coats had to be checked. By this time, she was fed up with him and said, "Can't I eat with my coat on if I want to?" And she walked on in. I did the same but removed my coat and laid it on a chair by the table. He immediately came and got it, carrying its fur collar like he had a hold of a dead skunk. Later, when I went to get it at the check counter, it was handed to me, and I thanked them and started out. The man at the check counter came running after us saying in good English, "You must pay. You must pay!" I did as I was told, as I was afraid not to; they throw people into jail there for no reason. In fact, I was seriously considering not ever taking my mom back into any Communist country, for, as I told her, "You're going to end up in jail!"

After the Iron Curtain came down, I again made many forays over into Eastern Europe, now enjoying the freedom to drive wherever I wished. The following are vignettes of some of my experiences.

One summer my mom and I drove from north to south and east to west in Czechoslovakia, as we wanted to see the entire country before it split into two separate countries. I then came back to Germany that summer with around a hundred unspent dollars in the Czech currency. Later, hearing that their current money would no longer be in use, I headed over one cold, snowy February weekend to one of the border towns to try and spend my leftover Korun. Finding a nice glass and china shop that was packed with people but that also had its doors locked, I managed to dart into the shop when the door opened for someone to leave. It was fun to just point at various dishes and say, "I want that and that and this," as everything was quite inexpensive.

On another trip to the Czech Republic, this time in November, I noticed pretty young girls standing by the highway at the outskirts of town trying to drum up business with some of the well-to-do Germans who were coming over the border. These girls were prostitutes who apparently had no other way of making a living. Since it was late fall, the weather was quite chilly, but these girls were dressed very scantily in nothing much but a little leather jacket. I felt very sad for them but also appalled that they had come to this.

Traveling in 1991 through East Germany, we were able to at last visit some of the cities we had heard so much about but had never been able to visit—Weimar, Dresden, Meissen, etc. We liked

Weimar the most, however. We especially enjoyed our hotel there. Called the "Elephant Hotel," it was so named because back in the past, elephant or mastodon bones were found there. Even the room keys were in the shape of an elephant. At this hotel, built in the 600s and, of course, remodeled over and over, such famous people as Bach, Wagner, Schiller, and even Hitler had stayed there. (We just hoped that we didn't spend the night in any room that Hitler may have enjoyed.)

Since I had brought along fifty copies of a Christian booklet written in German, I went out on the street one evening and handed them out. All of the people to whom I offered a booklet took it. This was probably the first time any of these Communist people had ever been given anything Christian telling them the way of salvation.

One of my favorite cities (which I visited often) was Karlovy Vary in the Czech Republic. The first time I went there I saw so many cars with American armed forces license plates that I thought there must be a conference going on. But as I walked downtown, I spotted the Americans. They were easy to tell from the natives, as they had their hands and arms full of boxes of glassware. (Some had even taken their babies out of their strollers and had their strollers filled with boxes of glass.) For after all, this is the city in which the famous Moser glass factory is located, in addition to all the other glass factories found throughout this city and country.

This is also a city of mineral waters and geysers. Many people come here just to drink the mineral water or to bathe in it. The downtown area is quite charming with a long walking street (no cars allowed in this area), which has a river running through the center with flowers on each side. In one building I saw a huge spray of water gushing clear up to the ceiling. It was one of the geysers found in the town, which had been enclosed in a building.

The walking street ends at the Pupp Hotel, a very famous and elegant hotel.

Even though I always headed for Karlovy Vary when going to the Czech Republic, there were many other places I enjoyed, for I found this to be a unique and beautiful country.

LESSON No. 4

GOD'S WORD IS ETERNAL

Various people and governments down through the ages have tried to destroy God's Word. They have attempted to do this by burning the Bible or by banning it. However, no one has ever been able to completely obliterate God's Word. It stands forever (Isaiah 40:8).

Because the Word of God is so important in getting people converted and in keeping people true to God, the devil would like to destroy it entirely. After all, the best way of getting people away from God or of getting them to disbelieve what God has said is to cause them to question or refute the Word of God. The devil did this in the very beginning when he asked Eve, "Has God said...?" (Genesis 3:1).

Everything that people have done, however, to destroy the Word of God has always come to naught—even in the Communistic countries. The leaders and secret police were obviously unaware of the different people who smuggled Bibles into their countries and of the various ways the Bibles were being brought in. One individual, Brother Andrew, would pray, "Lord, you made blind eyes see; now make seeing eyes blind." And this obviously happened, as the guards at the country's borders never found the Bibles Brother Andrew brought in.

It was with much trepidation, however, that I headed out with my Bibles—Bibles that were intended for people in a Communist country where all the Bibles had been confiscated. However, as has already been stated, the Lord kept the guards from even coming into our seating compartment.

There have been many stories down through the ages of how God has protected His Word. For instance, one missionary to

Burma, Adoniram Judson, who was in prison for many years in solitary confinement, found much comfort in a tattered old yellow pillow in which he had hidden a copy of the Word of God. And all the time he was imprisoned, God protected His Word so the guards never found it. That Bible, then, became his greatest treasure.

And there are many other stories of how people have managed to get the Bible into a place where it was not allowed. But all through the ages God's Word has survived.

CHAPTER 4

IN THE LAND OF WINTER, BUT NEVER CHRISTMAS

When we landed at the airport, (in November 1983) snow was all over the ground. I would have been disappointed if there hadn't been, as my mental picture of Russia always included snow. It was November, and Moscow had had ten inches of snow already.

After landing, we went immediately to customs. Getting through customs was a unique experience, as each person had to stand, one at a time, in front of a young Russian soldier who stared first at your passport and then at you. You felt rather like you were facing a single firing squad as the minutes passed by, and he continued to stare at you, unsmiling and deathly silent. Finally, if you didn't appear to be a threat to their Communist society, you were allowed to pass on into another room, where you retrieved your bags and had them x-rayed for contraband (contraband being, of course, things such as Bibles, comic books, and pornography).

As soon as all of our group safely made it through customs, we climbed aboard a large Russian bus to be taken to our hotel.

Our hotel was quite modern. Each room even contained a color television set, although I never could get mine to work.

When we had gotten situated in our rooms, my mother announced that she was thirsty. Since the travel literature had said that the tap water was unsafe to drink, I decided to buy a bottle of mineral water. Having noticed an icebox standing by the lady who kept the keys (on each floor there was a lady ensconced behind a desk to whom you turned in your keys each time you left your room). I approached her and asked for a bottle of water. When I went to pay for it, however, I found she would not take my American dollars or German marks, and I had no Russian rubles, since we had just arrived, and the hotel bank was already closed for the day. I tried to explain to her that I would pay her as soon as I got some money changed, but to my consternation she understood none of my "jabbering." I soon found myself in a position similar to the criminal, as I began having to sneak around, hoping to avoid "the keeper of the keys." Every time she spotted me, she demanded her money. At least I understood that much. Whatever else she was saying (whether she was threatening to have me arrested or something worse), I fortunately did not understand. I certainly felt much happier the next day when I got some money changed and "the keeper of the keys" was paid.

The name of our hotel was Belgrade I. My mother and I discovered one evening when we were let out of a taxi that just across the street was a hotel called Belgrade II. And this is the one we entered. We knew that we were on the right street, as the buildings looked familiar, but somehow the lobby of the Belgrade II Hotel appeared completely different. We were thankful that we discovered we were in the wrong hotel while we were still in the lobby and did not get involved with "the keeper of the keys" in a hotel that was not our own.

After a good night's rest, we were to begin our sightseeing tour the next morning. However, I became panicky when I discovered I was missing an important document given to us the night before to keep for money transactions. I had visions of being thrown into a Russian jail for the rest of my life. I was very much relieved when I found the document was with my passport, which was being kept by the hotel receptionist!

Our sightseeing tour took us to all the usual attractions—the Kremlin, Red Square, St. Basil's Cathedral, etc. Red Square we discovered to be neither red nor square. It was a long rectangular area going uphill from the street and Moscow River below. At one end were Lenin's Tomb and the Russian Historical Museum. At the other end was St. Basil's Cathedral. All along one side of Red Square was the beautiful red brick wall of the Kremlin. Inside the Kremlin were four Russian Orthodox cathedrals. For a country that claims to be atheistic, their seat of government came well-equipped with places of worship! None of them were used as actual places of worship, however, but were museums when we were there.

Breaking away from the tour group one evening, my mother and I went on our own to visit the GUM state-owned department store. It was a crisp, cold evening as we entered through the large side entrance of the store to mingle among some 350,000 people who daily shop in GUM. One of the people in our group described GUM as looking like a big, dirty railroad station with a balcony. Actually, this is not just a single department store, but rather many different stores under one roof. There were three floors but no elevators or escalators. Neither were there any places to rest one's tired feet or body, as was shown by the yellowish walls, which were tinged with black where countless tired bodies had leaned up against them seeking a moment's rest. Each floor was divided into two long, wide corridors, which were lined with small shops. Once inside the shops, it was difficult to even get up to a counter to see what they had to sell because of the crowds of people lined up inside. Once a person found something to buy, he or she had to first show the clerk the item wanted, then pay for it before he or she could actually hold it in his or her hands. And the sales personnel figured the bill on beaded abacuses!

Just inside the entrance to the building was a beer dispensing machine with a single glass from which everyone was supposed to drink. And throughout the store were found many ice cream vendors. They seemed to be doing a brisk business, as we brushed past many ice cream cones in all stages of being devoured.

After making a purchase of two bottles of perfume, we decided to head back to our hotel. Coming out of the warm store into the cold Russian night, we developed countless goose bumps as we walked along the street shivering. Everything was dark as we headed toward a large thoroughfare where we thought we could catch a taxi. Although it was getting close to Christmas, and all the shops in Western Europe had been gaily decorated with religious symbols of the season, there was not a single Christmas decoration anywhere in Moscow. We saw only the ruby red stars glowing in the night, which were placed on top of Communist government buildings. The whole scene—snow everywhere but no sign of Christmas—reminded me of C. S. Lewis's, land of Narnia, in which there was always winter but never Christmas.

We placed ourselves in a strategic position near the street and began trying to hail a taxi. Several actually did stop, but upon noticing our destination (I had a card with the name of our hotel in my hand for purposes of better communication as I can only speak two words of Russian, *yes* and *no*), the answer was always "nyet" (no). As the time passed, and we got colder and colder, I suggested that we walk over to the Rossia Hotel, supposedly the largest hotel in the world. I thought it might be easier to catch a taxi at a hotel. But such was not the case. When I tried to ask someone for help, no one spoke any of the languages that I speak.

Finally, an important-looking gentleman came out of the hotel and started directing the placement of luggage in a car near us. I approached him, asking him in both English and German if he could help us get a taxi. Although he did not understand either language, he did understand the word "taxi" and so proceeded to get one for us. I greatly appreciated his help and was thankful to at last be able to plop down on a comfortable seat in a warm car. However, I was amazed when the man who had gotten us the taxi hopped into the front seat. And then we sped away into the night, not knowing if we were really headed for our hotel, and with the man in the front seat talking a "blue streak" of Russian to us. Finally, we actually did arrive at our hotel, and as I got in my purse to get some rubles for payment, the man in the front seat indicated that he would pay for the taxi. As I thanked him and started to shake his hand, he grabbed my hand and began to profusely kiss it! I have often wondered since just who this man was, what he was saying to me in the taxi, and why he did what he did.

On Saturday afternoon our tour group was taken inside the Kremlin to a ballet, which was being performed by some of the members of the Bolshoi Ballet Group. Since the ballet was being performed in a Communist country, it, quite naturally, was about the struggle of the classes. It depicted an onion that was trying to overthrow some cherries. The ballet was being performed especially for children, and so the audience was composed of mostly children, some of whom looked to be as young as two or three years of age. Many of the school-age children were wearing their school uniforms—little girls with black dresses and white aprons and little boys in blue suits, but all of them with red scarves around their necks, signifying their membership in a

Young Pioneer Group. Many of the girls had long pigtails with big white bows in their hair.

The Russian women in the audience were dressed up for the ballet in their best long-sleeved dresses or in nice sweaters and skirts. But with these, they all wore boots! (Some of our group that had gone shopping on their own one day ran into a wedding party leaving a hotel, and the bride and her attendants all had on long wedding attire—but with boots! On these cold, snowy, and/ or mushy-wet streets, boots were a necessity.) Only the tourists had on slacks at the opera, so it was easy to identify the foreigners from the Russian women.

During the performance, I watched the people who were sitting around me, but especially the children. I have never seen a more rapt audience. They were sitting on the edges of their seats quietly taking in every movement. Of course, the scenery and the costumes were just fantastic, and the dancing was exceptionally well done.

The last evening we were in Moscow, our group visited a Russian Orthodox monastery. It was another cold night with snow all over the ground. As we walked along the sidewalk, we saw Russian mothers pulling their children on sleds. In the distance, a dog was barking. Otherwise, everything was silent. (Russian motorists were not allowed to honk their horns at night.) This quiet, dark street, piled high with snow and with a full moon overhead illuminating the golden onion domes of the monastery, was my idea of a typical Russian scene and was the conclusion of an interesting and eventful time spent in Moscow.

After such an interesting and memorable time spent in the Russian capital, one would think our flight aboard our Russian-built plane back to Germany would be uneventful. But such was not the case. The first problem we encountered was that of unassigned seats. The Germans, who had crowded around the exit doors of the airport, got the choice seats, and, therefore, my mom and I didn't get to sit together. In fact, we each had to sit in one of those uncomfortable middle seats.

But a second, and far worse, problem was that there seemed to be no nonsmoking section on the plane. People lighted up wherever they sat, so we had smoke beside us, in front of us, behind us, and across the aisle. After a while I was having a difficult time breathing and asked my neighbors on either side of me if they would mind not smoking. Their answer was to light up another cigarette, and these cigarettes were longer than the usual ones.

Mentioning my problem to Mom, who was sitting just in front of me, we prayed together that God would handle this situation. Suddenly we encountered some turbulent weather, causing the plane to drop in altitude and shake violently. We were a bit frightened for a while, but then we noticed that the "Fasten your seat belt" and "No Smoking" signs flashed on. And from then on we had no more problems with cigarette smoke. We then realized that God had used this as a way to answer our prayers.

LESSON NO. 5

FOLLIES OF COMMUNISM

While living in Europe, I was able to travel to many of the Communist countries, and I found some similar distinctive characteristics in each country. The most pronounced characteristic seemed to be the look of despair that was etched on the faces of many of the native people. But this came as no surprise to me, since conditions in these countries were rather bleak. Most people had to work hard for a very small amount of compensation and, therefore, had little in the way of worldly goods.

A second characteristic was that of distrust. Since a good Communist could turn over the names of people who were rebelling or going against Communistic laws, people tended to have a natural distrust toward others, sometimes even members of their own family. For instance, those who wished to attend an evangelical-type church rather than one of the state-run churches had to meet together secretly in a private home. But since this was clearly against the law, those people were actually risking their very lives in order to worship God, and, therefore, were very careful about telling others where they were meeting.

A third characteristic of Communism was that of a lack of motivation. Since most businesses, factories, land, and real estate were state-owned, the people had little desire to work vigorously because they were not working for themselves and because they would get paid regardless of whether they sold anything or not. When people are not allowed to make their own choices as to what their store will sell, or whether they could butcher their own livestock, for instance, they tend to become less aggressive in their business practices. Consequently, there was always a shortage of many important supplies, such as gasoline, meat, milk, etc., which resulted in long lines of people waiting for these items.

A fourth, and perhaps the worst, characteristic of Communism was the lack of personal freedom. For instance, people did not have the right to worship God as they pleased. Instead of having the wide choice of houses of worship that we enjoy here in the United States, there were only the state-run churches dominated by the Communist Party. Since the pastors and priests of these churches were basically told what they could and could not say, they became mere puppets of a godless government.

Another basic right is the freedom of speech, which, again, was disallowed in the Soviet Union. For instance, people could not speak out against the government or its leaders without experiencing a swift reprisal. We know that many people were condemned to live out their lives in Siberia because of something they had said or had done against the government.

The right to travel at will was another missing freedom. Good party members might be allowed to visit another country, but this was not so for the average person.

Thus, what I observed first-hand in visiting the various Eastern European countries that were under a Communistic-type government is that Communism only works well for the favored few at the top of the political spectrum. But for the average person, Communism was a millstone hung around his or her neck.

CHAPTER 5

BREAKING DOWN WALLS

The few times I went through the infamous Berlin Wall, I found the experience daunting. But getting out of East Berlin was more difficult than getting in. For instance, at Checkpoint Charley, when leaving, we had to get off the bus and line up all facing forward, according to the numbers they had previously given us, while they checked our faces with our passports. We felt like we were facing a firing squad! Then after we were all back on the bus, the East German soldiers came with a device that looked something like a moving dolly with a rectangular mirror on its bottom, and they ran this all around under the edge of the bus to see if anyone was hanging on underneath. Next, the bus was required to go through a very narrow passageway, reminding one of a car wash, which had all sorts of detecting devices in and around it. At last, we were free to pass on over to the western side! Everyone gave a sigh of relief when we knew we were out.

Thus, in 1989 I was overjoyed when I heard the news that the wall was coming down! One weekend my mom and I flew up to Berlin, bought a cold chisel, and taxied out to the wall to begin our work of helping to dismantle it. The atmosphere that day was like a circus or a state fair, with some people chipping at the wall, others taking pictures, and yet others just walking up and down picking up small pieces of the wall that various people had dropped.

One man had even brought a step ladder and sledgehammer, so he was able to break off some large pieces. We ended up buying several pieces from him, as it turned out to be a daunting task to chip good-sized pieces from the wall. Being made of solid concrete, the wall was thirteen feet high and ninety-six miles long and was, therefore, not easy to break.

It seemed incredible that people were even handling the wall, as I remembered from former times seeing the barbed wire at the top and the guardhouses that housed people with guns ready to shoot anyone who got too close to the wall. In fact, in the area behind the place we were working was a cross that had been set up to commemorate those hundreds who had died trying to get across the wall to freedom.

Since walls can represent a hindrance to freedom, safety, and a normal way of life, I want to tell about several kinds of walls that I experienced in my living in Europe and in my working for God.

One type of wall is that of drug addiction. One summer when I was vacationing in the States I heard on television about a park in Zürich, Switzerland, known as "Needle Park." This was a place where young people who were drug addicts would be given free needles, and, therefore, youths from all over Europe were congregating there. (Free needles were given out with the hope of cutting down on the transmittal from shared needles of diseases such as hepatitis and AIDS.)

Once back in Europe, I decided one holiday to load up my car with helpful religious materials to take down to "Needle Park" and give out to the addicts. I remembered Zürich from past vacations as a beautiful, clean city having a large pristine lake at one end of the town and tall, modern buildings bordering on parks in the center of town. I was, therefore, shocked when I saw the area around "Needle Park." Here the city streets were dirty and littered with trash. I drove around trying to find a hotel that had a parking garage, as I did not want to park out on the street. I finally did find the ideal hotel. Even though very expensive, it was located just across the street from the park and had a place to park underground.

My mom and I were given a room on the sixteenth floor. Since it was already late afternoon, we decided to wait until the next day before giving out our literature. Looking down from our window, we watched the activities over in the park. A river ran along the side of the park, and beside the river was a brick ledge about two feet high. We noticed some of the young people lying on the ledge asleep. Evidently, they had been able to purchase drugs and were now feeling the effects of them. We noticed many tables on which there was a type of Bunsen burner that was used to liquefy the drugs. These tables were manned by those selling the drugs. We watched until all the lights on the tables went out, and the park became completely dark.

When we awoke the next morning, we looked down once again on the park from our window. Since it was early Sunday morning, very few people were there. I did spot, though, a Red Cross boat floating down the river that surrounded the park. And as I watched, the Red Cross worker hauled a body out of the river. No doubt it was one of the addicts that had earlier been lying on the ledge and had fallen into the river, probably sometime in the night.

Around noon my mom and I took our literature and went over to the park. We were the only nondruggies there other than the person in the small camper who was giving out the free needles. The scene was incredible. Many young people were in the park, most injecting themselves with drugs, some in their fingers or legs, because the veins in their arms had all collapsed due to heavy drug use. Some were asleep on the ledge by the river, and others were just wandering around glassy-eyed and not alert. Still others were pawing at the ground like dogs, evidently unable to purchase any drugs and, therefore, very nervous.

For quite a while we stood at the gate to the entrance of the park, and from there we handed out our literature. Since it was lunchtime, we noticed that most of the addicts coming in were eating junk food such as cookies and candy, rather than anything substantial and beneficial. My mom, having a mother's heart, was already planning out our next trip to the park, which would include a trunk load of sandwiches and apples.

After we had passed out all our literature, we headed back to our hotel. The next morning we awoke to find snow all over the ground, as this was in January. We noticed very few people in the park as we left and headed out for home. Sadly, we never did go back again, as the park was closed down for addicts shortly after we had been there.

A slightly different type of wall involved weather. One year my mom and I booked a tour for the Middle East, visiting countries such as Greece, Egypt, Syria, Turkey, and Israel. We took a train from Nürnberg, Germany, where I was then teaching, up to Frankfurt, from where we would be flying. Staying overnight in Frankfurt, we took a taxi the next morning out to the airport. As we drove along the Autobahn to the airport, I noticed what seemed like walls on each side of the highway. "That's funny," I thought, "I've never noticed any walls here before." Then I realized this was not walls; rather, it was heavy fog.

When we got to the airport, it was very crowded with tour groups and individuals milling around waiting for their flights to be called. But because of the heavy fog, no flights were leaving or arriving. After waiting nearly half a day, I began praying that the fog would lift, and to my delight, our flight was soon called. On this particular 747 were three tour groups and a number of Greek people, since we would be going to Athens first.

As we lifted up through the heavy fog, not a sound could be heard on the plane—all was deadly silence. Before long, however, we broke through the heavy clouds, seeing for the first time that day bright sunshine! A very jubilant steward then announced over the intercom, "Folks, this is the only intercontinental flight to leave Frankfurt today!"

Sometimes walls can be barriers or problems that the devil puts up. Such was the case with our trip to Budapest, Hungary.

After the Iron Curtain had come down, I read in our armed forces newspaper, *The Stars and Stripes*, about a man who had been a professor in a university in Hungary. He had lost his job and his home and was now having to live at the train station in Budapest. I told Mom, who was living with me in Germany at that time, that I was going to drive to Budapest over my Christmas holidays and take that poor man some food. I had planned to load up the trunk of my car with bags of potatoes and apples, canned hams, etc. She, however, felt that it would be wiser if we drove over there and checked the situation out first.

So on Christmas Eve Day, we headed out. Instead of all the food I had earlier planned to take, I now had, instead, one hundred copies of a religious magazine in the Hungarian language, which I wanted to give out to people I would encounter on the streets. Evidently, the devil didn't want this to happen and so tried to stop our getting there with various frightening situations and problems.

While driving on the Autobahn through the foothills of the Alps, I started to pass a long truck. Because the foothills were covered with snow, and the highway was somewhat slushy, I took my time getting around the truck. Glancing up into my rearview mirror, I spotted a car, its headlights on, barreling down upon me at a very high rate of speed. I realized they were going to pass me in the passing lane and so pulled over as close to the truck as I could get. (There were no speed limits at this time on the Autobahns in Germany, and this car was probably traveling at 100 miles per hour or more.) Fortunately, they passed me safely, but I was so shaken up I had to stop at the next Rastplatz (resting area) until my heart stopped pounding, and I could calm down a bit.

Finally able to travel on, I headed out. Since it was beginning to grow dark, we decided to stop for the night at a hotel on the outskirts of Vienna, Austria. Once in our room, Mom lay down on the bed to rest awhile. I suggested that we needed to eat our Christmas Eve dinner down in the hotel restaurant before turning in for the night. So Mom asked me to help her up off the bed. Taking her by one hand, I pulled her up. Screaming with pain, my mom yelled, "Oh, my leg!" Not knowing what was wrong with her leg, I helped her down the stairs and into the dining room, where we ordered our meal and began to eat. But Mom was in such pain that we couldn't finish our meal, and so I paid the bill, and we went back upstairs to our room.

When we got to the room, I massaged Mom's leg, soaked it in warm water, gave her an aspirin, and prayed. But nothing seemed to help. Shortly after falling asleep, I was awakened by hearing my mom moaning. Finally I said, "Tomorrow we will head back to Germany, where I can take you to your doctor." She was silent a while before answering, "No, we will go on."

The next morning the desk clerk allowed me to drive my car up to the front door of the hotel, and then he helped me get Mom into the backseat of the car, where she could lie down. Having never been in Vienna before, Mom was in too much pain to really enjoy seeing the sights as I drove her through the city.

It was late afternoon when we finally arrived in Budapest. This was Christmas Day, and snow was all over the ground, truly giving us a white Christmas. Finding a large hotel at the edge of town, I asked, when registering, if they had a wheelchair available. They did, and I was then able to get Mom up to our room. That evening we had room service bring us our Christmas dinner, and then we went to bed and tried to sleep.

The next day, Monday, was a European holiday called Boxing Day. I headed out toward downtown with my one hundred magazines, intending to give them all out before returning to the hotel. The magazines went fast, and considering that Hungary and the other East European countries had been under Communism for the past fifty years with little or no chances to obtain religious materials, this in itself was a miracle! But I found out the biggest miracle of the day when I got back to the hotel. My mom said that the pain in her leg went away right after I left. We never did find out what was wrong with her leg, and her doctor, after examining it, couldn't find anything wrong either. We both felt, however, that this may have been a ploy of Satan to keep me from giving out those one hundred magazines to people who desperately needed to hear the message of salvation.

Language can also be a barrier, because it's impossible to communicate with someone whose language you don't speak. But a little knowledge can also be a dangerous thing. At least that is what I discovered as I attempted conversing with the natives while traveling and living abroad.

Once in Yugoslavia I found out by trial and error that sometimes one's own native tongue is the simplest way to get people's attention. At a filling station near Belgrade where I had stopped to get twenty liters of gas for my car, I started with the language I know best (other than English), German, as many Yugoslavs, especially near the Austrian border, speak German.

When the attendant stared blankly at me, I shifted into Italian. I got a blank stare. Next I used my French, "Parlez vous francais?" No answer. Lastly, in vain, I tried Spanish. When no answer was forthcoming, I turned to my mother, who was traveling with me, and told her that I simply did not know what to do as I did not know any of the Slovakian languages. She suggested that I write out the number of liters I wanted, as numbers are generally the same in every language. At this point the attendant, overhearing us conversing in English, got into action and said in English, "Oh, do you want twenty liters of gas?" I had forgotten to ask the man if he spoke English!

Several times I was complimented on how well I could speak English. One day some young American soldiers hurriedly approached me on a street in Heidelberg, Germany, first asking me if I could speak English and then proceeding to ask for the directions to the train station. After getting the directions, they complimented me on how well I spoke English, and before I could even tell them I was a fellow American, they were gone, no doubt telling one another as they hurried on to the train station how lucky they were to find a German who could speak such good English.

Several times I have found the results of speaking English quite humorous, if not even a bit disastrous, however. Once as I was wandering around the streets of Athens, Greece, I chanced upon a store that carried telephone parts, and in the window was a telephone insulator. Knowing how delighted some of my mother's insulator collector customers from her antique shop would be to have an insulator from Greece, I entered the store and asked if I could buy the insulator in the window. It turned out that their knowledge of English was not too good, and before I left I about had a telephone installed, although where it would have been installed I have no idea.

It really does pay to consult a language dictionary occasionally. After a particularly delicious meal in a German restaurant, my friend and I asked the waitress if we could have the recipe for the salad dressing, which was so unusual and so good. She nodded her assent and later came bringing us the recipe, all written out in German, of course. When I got home, I decided to make the recipe. However, I did not have the last ingredient, "eine wenig Magie." So I hurried to the corner grocery store and began looking in the spice section for some "Magie." When I could not find it among the spices, I went home, looked the word up in my German dictionary and found it was "a little magic."

Fortunately, most Europeans are rather understanding and even seem to have a healthy respect for Americans who try to speak their language.

I had ordered a room for my mom and myself one night in France and was real proud of my ability to ask in French if, first, they had a vacant room for two people with two beds, then how much the cost for the night would be. The desk clerk had dutifully answered all my questions, but upon telling me the price, he suddenly broke into English saying, "and that includes breakfast." He had to let me use a lot of poor French before demonstrating to me how well he could speak English.

I was not that lucky in Italy, though. I used my best Italian to ask in an antique shop if they had any old bridle bits. (My dad had quite an extensive collection of them). The antique dealer smiled at me and said patronizingly, "Io capisco solamente Italiano"—— "I only understand Italian." Wow, was my ego ever deflated.

I know I had used the correct Italian, too, as an Italian friend had told me what to say. Of course, there are occasions when a person does use the wrong word. The fact that one does not end up with more serious consequences shows the patience and perseverance on the part of Europeans and Americans alike. For instance, once when my friend asked in a restaurant for "ein Beutel Wasser," the waiter actually did bring her the bottle of drinking water she thought she had asked for, rather than the bag of water she had in reality asked for. And once when I asked in a German garage for four bicycles for my car instead of four tires, the clerk patiently told me she did not understand me, rather than wheeling out four new bicycles.

Americans, too, have to learn to deal with misspoken English. In one of the fanciest restaurants in Vienna, Austria, I pointed to an entrée on the menu and asked what it was "auf Englisch." He replied in polite, but final terms, "That is dog, Madame." I gulped, looked up and down the menu until I found the words, "Chicken a la King" written out in English and proceeded to order that.

I have found one surefire method, when all words fail, however, and that is to act out what you want to say. I talked for fifteen minutes once to a man in Romania—he speaking in Romanian and I in English. Most of what we said, we acted out.

Maybe acting out what you want to say is the safest course to take. At any rate, I've found it isn't the best idea to pretend you're understanding what the person is saying in his or her language if you really don't. I was trying to understand an elderly lady who was sitting at my table in a German restaurant. I didn't understand too much of what she was saying, and I kept saying, "bitte," the German equivalent for "please repeat." I noticed her voice kept getting louder and louder. Finally, I had to tell her I was an American and did not understand what she was saying. She then said to me in perfect English, "Oh, I thought you were deaf!"

LESSON NO. 6

PERSISTENCE PAYS

We learned from the several severe problems we experienced in traveling to Hungary that the devil will try to stop anything that will bring glory to God or get sinners saved. In fact, any time a person who is doing God's work experiences strange problems, this is a clear sign the devil is behind it. But if a person simply holds on and doesn't give up, nothing the devil does will be lasting. God will always triumph in the end.

The devil is very persistent, though, and if he can't do anything to stop the person's God-work, then he'll attack someone or something close to that person, as he did my mom. We never found out what caused the horrible pain in my mom's leg (possibly it could have been from sitting too long in one position in the car), but the pain was very real and almost caused us to turn around and head back home. However, Christians need to learn to be as persistent as the devil is.

Many times people can lose the answer to their prayer just short of victory. They may pray for healing, and when it doesn't happen right away, they give up. Or they may ditch a certain project because everything seems to be going against their getting it accomplished. It's important to remember that God has His own time schedule. In fact, He many times answers prayer just before a deadline occurs. He may do this to test our faith and our persistence.

So when my mom said, "We'll not turn back, but we'll go on," we had half of the victory already won. And actually (even though my mom's leg still bothered her somewhat), from that point on we had no further problems. Therefore, it's important to remember that when we encounter strange problems we need to do two things: pray as though everything is up to God and work as though everything is up to us, and then never give up!

CHAPTER 6

INSIDE POLAND

This is a letter my mother wrote to her sister after a trip to Poland.

Dear Zola,

I will tell you some about our trip to Poland. I was surprised to find Poland so flat—a lot of its interior is actually below sea level—for most of the European countries are generally mountainous, give or take one or two like Holland. There are a few not-too-tall mountains lying along its border with Czechoslovakia. So except for some mining in this area (they mine coal, iron, and silver), Poland is largely agricultural. And we found this out at every meal! We almost always had a salad plate of shredded carrots, celery, cabbage, often beets, and, of course, potatoes. The potatoes were usually served as a heavy glob—mashed—but unwhipped and unseasoned. Sometimes down around the city of Krakau, they were served as french fries. In the area below sea level the farms are crisscrossed with drainage ditches, and we saw many lakes near the northern part of Poland.

Getting back to Polish food, though, we were always served a bowl of soup to begin our meal, delicious and a meal in itself. We had meat with our potatoes, usually pork, but sometimes beef or fish, and always very tender and well-prepared. Mushrooms were used much with meat dishes, as they harvest gobs of these from their forests. (Since mushrooms have an adverse effect on me, I usually scraped them off my meat; now, come to think of it, I'm glad I did, as I remember that whenever the bus's portable toilets needed to be emptied, they always stopped at the forested area to do it.) Our dessert was usually a delicious pastry—part cake and part whipped or sour cream with a very flaky pie-crust bottom, which made it hard for me to eat with a fork, and I usually ended up with a flaky mess on my plate. For breakfast, besides strong coffee, we had cheese and sliced Polish ham or summer-type sausage and round hard rolls, and once in a while sweet poppy seed rolls and apple juice. It was a real treat to have orange juice, as citrus fruit and such things as bananas are among their foodstuff shortages. In Warsaw we saw people lined up for nearly a block waiting to buy oranges from a street dealer.

We stayed in their Socialist government hotels—a line of hotels called Orbis—and what we had to eat in these hotels was not what the people out on the street could get to eat.

Food went first to these government hotels, and other hotels, cafes, and stores went without these foodstuffs. So, whenever I left any food on my plate (and I did quite often as they gave you ample amounts), I felt like a criminal, knowing that the Polish people in general couldn't even buy a lot of these things, particularly meats. Jane and I pulled out a couple bananas to eat as a snack while waiting in the Warsaw train station on our arrival to Poland, and I saw a young Polish boy looking so longingly at my banana that I whispered to Jane, "Do you suppose these people do not have bananas?" Later we were to learn from our Polish tour guide that this was so. It made me feel so ashamed that we had eaten those bananas in front of that kid, but, of course, we did not know this then. This is Communism! And this is the reason that Lech Walesa got the Polish people to revolt—foodstuff shortages and continuing higher prices. The Polish people are almost 100 percent behind Walesa and against the Soviets. They never miss a chance to poke fun at or give the Soviets a dig. They are required to study Russian in their schools, but none of them will speak it unless required to do so. Stalin gave Warsaw their Palace of Cultures Building, located in downtown Warsaw. It is a tiered building (built like a wedding cake) with a tall top tower. The Poles call it "Stalin Gothic," and they say from its tower is the best place to view Warsaw, because then you won't have to view it! As Jane concluded, "They are a feisty people who won't tolerate being run over." The Catholic priest at one of their main monasteries said of Walesa, "He is not afraid of anything or anyone." Our guide said, "We think he will be president of Poland someday." The Polish people are pro-America and anti-Soviet.

Since the tour group we were with were all from the armed forces bases in West Germany, we fell right in with these Poles' way of thinking and felt a bond of comradeship with them. Soon we were all buying and wearing Solidarity pins, which our Polish guide furnished us, but with the warning that we should not have them on when we went through customs as we departed Poland, as the Socialist officials might not take this too well.

Poland was the only one of these Communist European countries that Jane had not visited, so it took priority over other places to visit over her Easter vacation. But what a time we had getting there! First, if we took the West German Scheffler tour (the only one we could find that was going to Poland at this time) we would have to relinquish our passports to them for a whole month, and that would mean that we could only travel around Germany all this time. Also, to take the Scheffler tour you would have to be on their tour bus all night the first night traveling through West Germany and most of East Germany to get to the first stopover (Dresden), and the ride is too tiresome, cold, and you really don't get any sleep, wearing you out for any sightseeing the next day. So we decided we would go to Poland on our own. That proved to be a mistake!

On the first free day Jane had from school (President's Day), we got up real early and went to Bonn, where the consulates are located, to get our Polish visas (a ten-hour ride round-trip) only to find out that the Polish Consulate was located in Cologne (another one hour drive, at least) and that the consulate closed at two o'clock (it was nearing one thirty then); so no way! Next we tried to get the American Express Tour Bureau to help us. They informed us that it would take them a couple of weeks to get a visa for us and that we first would have to have paid-up hotel vouchers in order to get visas. Then if we couldn't get a visa, we would lose a percentage of our hotel money. (Hotels are high in Poland, the Communists making this so purposely so as to get the hard currencies of the Western countries.) We didn't want to risk losing a lot of money, so we decided we would just have to go someplace else other than Poland. By now it was too late to get on the Scheffler tour if we had wanted, as they had a booking deadline of four weeks before departure.

Jane had never been in Andorra, that little country up in the Pyrenees Mountains between Spain and France, and I had never been in Spain; so we decided we would go this route instead. We would have to go to Andorra by way of Spain, as this mountain road would not be travelable this time of year from France. Then we learned that because of drugs and sex crimes that had gotten out of control, even by the Spanish police, that our armed forces in Spain were warning all armed forces personnel stationed in Spain and also American tourists that it was no longer safe to travel around in Spain. So there went our Spanish trip!

Next we decided to get Eurorail train passes and go to Hungary via Vienna, but we found out that Budapest would be having a big spring festival at this very time, and all the hotels would be filled. Jane was not too eager to go there anyway, as she had been there a couple of times already.

Well, we could take the car and just leisurely drive around in France. Then Jane discovered her water pump was leaking, and she would not have the time to get it repaired. Anyway, Jane did not want to drive, as she said that way would not be any relaxing vacation for her, and she was in need of some relaxation from the stresses of school. What now?

One morning I awoke with this going through my head, "All things are possible if you believe." We both wanted to go to Poland, and I believed there was still a way to get there if we kept trying. We could go to Cologne and get our visas and call Poland direct and make our own hotel reservations and then take it from there. Jane agreed and asked me to call the Polish Consulate, which was closed during the hours she would be out of school; so it was up to me to do it. Finally I got hold of the consulate and found the man could not speak English (only just a very little), and I could not speak Polish and very limited German. But somehow I did find out we could get our visas the very same day if we were at the Communist Orbis Office at eight thirty in the morning. The guy even tried to spell out in English letters the Orbis address we were to come to. When Jane saw the spelled-out address, she declared that was not a German name for a street, so she rejected it. This caused us a lot of trouble later on up there, as he had only the first letters wrong.

Jane got permission from the school to be gone one day, and we took the train to Cologne and stayed in a very expensive hotel right in downtown Cologne next to the famous Cologne Cathedral and across the street from the train station. For some reason neither one of us slept, but, even so, it was better to be safe in a hotel room than out on the street or sitting in the train station all night. For when we checked our luggage at the train station the next morning we saw a youngish-looking man sitting there with a fresh head wound that was bleeding down on his coat collar and all through his hair, evidently having been wounded out on the street overnight. We tried to find the police so the man could get medical help but couldn't find any, and we had to be at that Orbis office if we were to get what we came for. Cologne, by the way, is a city of over a million people; in such a large city, much crime would take place.

Taking a taxi to a Polorbis Office, the Communist tourist bureau outside of Poland, we got our visa forms all filled out and stamped and then found out we could not get our visas from this office for several days, but they gave us the address of another office where we could get them that day. This was the branch office I had called. But the first office had given us the wrong street number (on purpose?), and the taxi couldn't find such a street number; so we had him take us to the main consulate. Here, as I said before, we found ourselves in a mass of wall-to-wall humanity, all pushing and shoving to get farther ahead in line. Here, we either waited sitting on hard benches or standing in line for six whole hours, with no time to go out and get a meal. I thought I'd go batty before we got out of there—tired and not having slept. Was Poland worth it?

Finally around three o'clock they started handing back the passports with the stamped-in visas. We were number 801, but they didn't take them by number. They had no order or organization to this procedure at all. It was whoever could push up first to the window and get his after the man in charge hunted through all those passports to find that particular one. The Communists try to make it as hard for a non-Communist as they can. Jane decided that we had come a long way and had a long way back, so she took things into her own hands and literally elbowed her way up to that window to get our passports. In the process the people nearly tore the handles off her purse and did tear a solid 14k gold bracelet right off her arm (we never did find it), but we finally had our visas!

Now we had to hurry back to that first Polorbis Office before it closed so we could get our hotel reservations set up. We walked blocks in a light drizzle before we could find a taxi stand. We got to the office only to be told, "It is too late for us to make you any hotel reservations. They had to be made two weeks ago." Now why did they not tell us that when we were first in there, as we had said we would go get our visas and be back right after to get the hotel reservations set up. I'm sure they do things like this just to irk non-Communists. Frustrated, we headed for the train station and home, getting in Monday night. Tuesday we got our plane reservations (Pan Am) and the required $30-a-day vouchers.

On Thursday, Jane started calling Polish hotels direct. She called at least five or six different ones both in Warsaw and Krakau. All she got was busy signals. Finally, upon one call a man answered. Jane asked, "Could we get a room in your hotel?" And she got, "This is no hotel. This is a private residence." Puzzled, Jane asked, "What have I got? I'm trying to call Poland." The reply was, "This is Copenhagen." Again she tried, and this time got someplace in Germany. After several other line-busy signals, I heard a loud "bang" in the hall, and I jumped up and ran to see what was the matter. There was the phone and guide books on the floor and Jane sitting there with tears in her eyes, completely exasperated. Here we were to fly out Saturday morning, and we could get no reservations, and from all we had learned, it was nigh onto impossible to get one after you got there. (We later learned that the phone system was all a mixed-up mess, even inside Poland, let alone long distance.) What were we to do? If we couldn't go, Jane could get only part of her plane money back.

I suggested, "Maybe, since we already have our visas, we might still be able to get on that Scheffler tour. Maybe they have some extra seats, or someone cancelled out. Why don't you call and see." Jane brightened with that possibility, but for now she only wanted to go to bed. She then went into her room and prayed about it.

The next morning before going to school, she called Scheffler Tours and got ahold of Mr. Scheffler himself. Finding out we had visas, he asked, "Can you be ready to leave this evening?" (They would be starting to pick up their tour people from various places around Germany that very Friday evening.) In the meantime, Mr. Scheffler had found that the names of all the tour people had already been given to East Germany, as required by that country. So we could not get in on that part of their trip. Since we already had plane tickets for Warsaw, however, he was able to work it out so we could fly to Warsaw and then take a train to meet their tour group at the first stopover across the border into Poland. We would then be with the group for the complete Polish tour. This was what we wanted in the first place, as we wanted to avoid that first long all-night ride and the last all-night ride back into Germany across Czechoslovakia.

W later on found out that it would have been almost impossible for us to have traveled around Poland on our own, not knowing any more than we did at the time. We feel that God did not let Jane get a hotel reservation purposely, as He had this better plan all in mind for us. And it was a lot cheaper than had we been on our own and without all the anxious hassle we would have had to endure had we been on our own! We believe that sometimes when things don't work out as you want them to, it isn't that God doesn't want you to do it, but, rather, He has a better way than your planned-out way. This is a lesson that we all need to keep in mind.

When we arrived at the Warsaw-Prague gate (this plane would touch down at Prague before landing at Warsaw) at the Frankfurt Airport, Mr. Scheffler had a Telex message there awaiting us that gave us detailed instructions as to what to do after arriving in Warsaw. First, we were to change some money over into Polish zlotys. (We did this at the official Orbis Bank at the airport, and they gave us only one-fifth as much for our dollar as the Polish tour guide gave the tour people.) Next, we were to take a bus for the central train station and catch the first fast train for the city of Poznan, where the tour group would be staying in the Orbis-Polonez Hotel.

When we arrived in Warsaw, a shuttle bus took the planeload of people from the plane to the airport building. As we left the bus to go into the building, we were greeted by a soldier with a hip pistol and a rifle, who carefully gave us the once-over. We had to go through a custom check here also, showing a paper form that stated how much foreign money we were bringing in with us. (It is a crime to take out more money than you've brought in—minus purchases—which will have to be declared upon leaving, and no zlotys can be taken out.) Somehow we always manage to be the last in the line going through these places, so when Jane lined up again to change money over, she had gotten up to the window when they slammed it shut in her face. So she had to start over at the back of another line.

We were soon to learn how nice the Polish people really were (that is, outside of the few Communist officials with whom we met). Hurrying out to a waiting city bus, Jane jumped on and asked the bus driver where we could get bus tickets. He spoke no English, so Jane asked, "Does anyone on here speak English?" One man answered her that he did. So she asked him where and how we could get bus tickets. He just reached into his pocket and pulled one out and handed it to her. She told him, "But I need two of them." He answered, "No problem," and pulled out another and gave it to her. He would not accept any money for them, and he even got up and gave me his seat. Then when he found out that we wanted to go to the main train station, he told us what we really wanted was not the main station, but the central one. Then he got off with us at the right place, carrying our one suitcase, and led us right up to the ticket window before he bid us good-bye.

Jane didn't think they gave us the right ticket; it was for a slow train, and Mr. Scheffler said for us to get the fast train, for it was going to be a five-hour ride even so. A black fellow just ahead of her, who also could speak English, came to her aid and helped her get supplement tickets for first class on a fast train. It turned out that he was going to take that same train to a college up in the area we were going to.(He was a student there from Africa.) He carried some of our luggage and took us to the waiting room. We had missed the first train we were supposed to have taken; now we would have to wait until eight in the evening for the next one. Our black friend told us he had to go make a phone call and would be back. The time came for the train to be there and the man wasn't back; we went out on the platform but couldn't read the signs to tell which train on which side of the platform to take, and there was no one there to help us who knew English. We were tired, cold, and now confused. About that time here came our black man down a flight of stairs. I never knew how glad I would be to see him! He informed us that our train had been cancelled, but another would come at eight thirty. We began another wait, but it was interesting just watching the Polish people.

Finally, our black friend got us on the right train and in an enclosed six-seat compartment. There was seemingly no heat on the train, and we got cold in the night; but the black man made us as comfortable as he could by pulling window curtains across the cold windows and seeing that the door was kept closed. And when it came time for us to get off, he told us when. Then he stood and waved to us as we made our way toward a taxi stand where we would get a ride to our Poznan Hotel. I'm sure God has angels to help you, and sometimes they may even be black!

Once in that long night ride, the conductor came around to punch tickets. He got very perturbed when Jane handed him the first two tickets and then her supplement tickets instead of all of them together. He came clear into the compartment, ranting and raving in Polish and pointing to the conductor stripe on his coat sleeve. Then he angrily folded the tickets together and thrust them down into Jane's hand while still ranting. We didn't know anything he was saying, so it didn't really bother us too much— just chalked it off as a sore-headed Communist.

It was one thirty in the morning when we finally crawled into the warm beds of our hotel. We had been up nineteen hours traveling by train, bus, foot, and plane! The German and Polish tour guides had waited up for us until 11:00 p.m., but when we had not shown up by that time they concluded we had gone on to Gdansk to meet them there. We probably would not have missed the first train to Poznan except we had been delayed for about an hour at the Frankfurt airport because of some incoming plane trouble. We never did find out what the trouble was; but when our plane finally was allowed to take off for Poland, Jane saw both a fire truck and an ambulance go out on the field.

With only a couple hours of sleep, we had to get up early the next morning to start our tour of the city of Poznan and our tour of the rest of Poland.

The next day we were to drive up to the city of Gdansk, which is located in the northern part of Poland on the Baltic Sea. On our way we stopped at Torun, which is situated on Poland's main river, the Vistula. Torun has more medieval monuments than any other city in Poland. It has 350 mostly Gothic-type structures. We visited one—a thirteenth century church, Church of Our Lady, and also saw the house where the astronomer Nicolaus Copernicus was born. I was the most impressed here with that wide blue river with myriads of white seagulls darting over it. Here we walked along it to a very wide flight of city steps leading to the old city gate.

Driving on after lunch at a restaurant, we arrived at Gdansk and stayed at the Orbis-Hevelius Hotel overnight. I'll always remember this particular hotel for the delicious poppy-seed rolls they had for breakfast. Gdansk is connected with two other cities—Sopot and Gdynia—along this Baltic coast; and like our twin cities of Minneapolis and St. Paul, these are called the "Tri-Cities." These cities, surprisingly, are actually located upon a rather high rocky crest, with the beaches down below. Sopot's beach was probably Poland's finest resort until the Poles here found out that a shipload of stuff deceitfully sent to Poland was actually bound for Russia, and they dumped the whole shipload in the sea here, and now it is too polluted for using for recreation. Of course, all three cities are connected with shipping and shipbuilding. And, as you know, at Gdansk was where that independent union, Solidarity, was born. We took a photo of the three-hundred-foot monument in the Lenin Shipyards here erected to honor the Poles who died in the 1970 and 1976 workers' uprisings.

You probably didn't know, as I didn't know, that Gdansk was formerly Danzig of old Prussia. Or that after World War I, it was designated a "free city." And when Hitler wanted it to be ceded to Germany, the Poles' refusal caused the first shot to be fired, starting World War II. Ninety percent of Gdansk was destroyed during World War II and had to be rebuilt.

We opted to have an hour's free time to look and shop around here rather than to go hear a big organ play at the Oliwa Cathedral. There were many jewelry shops (silver and amber mostly), one right after another, both up steps and down steps from the street level, along Mariacka Street in what is known as the Old Town. We visited many of them, but Jane decided that their things were too high and never bought a thing.

Driving on toward Warsaw, we stopped next at the city of Malbork and visited a medieval Teutonic Knights' castle. To enter the castle we had to cross on a wooden plank drawbridge over a moat. This was once the medieval headquarters of the Teutonic Knights' capital, and the castle, itself, is one of the largest Gothic fortresses in Europe.

Some Polish schoolboys were playing around near the bus parking lot, and they were curious as to our nationality. One asked, "Americano?" We nodded, but when we tried to engage them further in conversation, we found out they knew little English or German. We did wave and say, "Bye," to them; and they caught on and said, "Bye," back to us. Most of the Polish children we saw were pale and thin—probably undernourished—not robust-looking like our American or German children. We wished we had the chocolate candy to give them, which we brought along but which was locked up in our one suitcase.

We stayed two days in Warsaw. Warsaw is, of course, Poland's largest city, with one and a half million people. It was almost all destroyed during World War II, but was carefully restored, almost brick by brick and stone by stone, to its original forms. It has many pretty parks near the downtown area. One of them is dedicated to Chopin, Poland's own famous composer, and I think another was in honor of Paderewski, Poland's famous pianist. Other famous Poles were Arthur Bernstein and the Curies.

Here we stayed in the International Orbis Forum Hotel. It was around thirty stories high, had over 750 rooms and was advertised as being "air-conditioned." That last feature irked me, as I was always cold at night because we couldn't get the cool air completely turned off, and as a result, I just did not get one good night's sleep. There were other tour busloads of people here from other countries—Norway and Israel, to name a couple—so the hotel was pretty well filled up. All of the hotels we stayed in were four-star (deluxe) and were as nice as our better hotels in America. (They even had a big, new Holiday Inn in Krakau.) Poland seemed to have a lot of large, fine hotels. And as we went from one fine hotel to another, we naturally wondered why, when we had tried calling them earlier, we would only get a busy signal instead of someone answering. But as I said, God evidently had a hand in this!

I think it was at this Forum Hotel where, the last day, we were given a typical old-Polish meal: first we had "Pierogi," triangular noodle dough stuffed with cabbage, meat, and potatoes, and then boiled. They were pasty and heavy; this was followed by "Golabki," cabbage leaves stuffed with rice and beef and then baked. (I tried to indicate to the waitress that I only wanted one, but she thought I was asking for more and gave me two of them. Imagine all that cabbage! The dessert, as I remember, was the typical cream and cake pastry.

The waiters at these hotels all seemed to be running a second business on the sly in black-marketing money, Russian caviar, and Russian champagne. They would ask at every chance if you would like to change over some money, etc. Champagne and caviar were cheap in Poland—$3.00 for a bottle of champagne and $4.50 for caviar.

The last day at Warsaw turned out to be a beautiful, sunny day, and it was the first day of spring, and in Poland that is a school holiday, so all the college kids were out in force. They were having fun everywhere, particularly in the Market Place of the Old Town, where they were in groups and dressed in all sorts of crazy costumes. One fellow had a whole shower stall, complete with curtains and a water faucet at the top, around him, and he was trying to entice girls to come inside his curtains so he could kiss them. One girl had on sort of a clown costume, which had a large brown plastic hand holding a brown washrag at her rear end. There were hundreds of such kids and costumes! Instead of going into a cathedral on the square, I preferred to stay out on the street and watch the kids carrying on. Lech Walesa was in town at his Round-Table Meeting. (We passed the meeting building with a large white, red-lettered "Solidarity" banner on it, and our German tour guide was fearful the kids might start some kind of uprising.) If they did, I wanted to see it. But no such luck—they just had fun. (Poland, by the way, has the youngest population of any country in Europe, for over half of its population is under thirty-five years of age; the "oldies" having been killed off in World War II.

We had that afternoon off for shopping. The best places to shop are the state-run Cepelia Shops, which carry genuine folk crafts, and at a cheaper price than other shops. We bought a doll dressed in native costume of the Warsaw area, got a loaf of sweet poppy-seed bread at a department store, and bought two Easter sticks decorated with dry straw flowers around the upper two-thirds—an Easter item peculiar to Poland only. By this time I was so tired I wanted to go back to the hotel and just rest for once. I was still too tired to go down to eat dinner, so Jane went out to a little quick-lunch stand on the street and pointed to some soup (others were eating) to carry out. With the soup came slices of a heavy brown bread. The soup had pieces of beef and strips of potatoes in it in a sour cream and beef broth, and the bread tasted gritty. The soup was very good, but I declared the bread had sand in it. Jane tried to reassure me what I insisted was sand was actually just hard grains of barley or other grain, but I insisted it was sand, as it crunched like glass between my teeth. We finished this meal off with hunks of poppy-seed roll. Later in the night I got deathly sick and heaved up all my meal. We decided that maybe from now on we should not eat things from the street diners.

On our way to Krakau the next day, we stopped at the city of Czestochowa to see that famous fourteenth century painting *Our Lady of Czestochowa* (called the "Black Madonna") because she has been painted dark like Eastern peoples. The painting is the main attraction in this Pauline monastery, located on a hill above the city, called Gasna Gora (Hill of Light). This place is the most holy Catholic shrine in all of Poland, a country 95 percent Catholic. The painting is covered with silver and is only shown twice a day. The image itself wears a cloak covered with military honors. (The Poles don't find this the least bit odd. I reckon because they, themselves, are such a fighting people.) The image has two slashes on one cheek, reputedly inflicted by an enraged Tartar who found the painting getting heavier and heavier as he was trying to steal it. An adjoining room is filled with all sorts of gold and silver crosses and other treasures left there by grateful worshippers. The painting is said to have miraculous powers, and has been the object of veneration for centuries. There was even a pair of crutches left there by someone claiming healing. The priest who showed us around had lived one time in the United States of America, and so spoke English really well. He was also a clever one and joked a lot. He blessed everyone with a parting prayer for our safe journeys, and couldn't resist adding, "particularly if they are flying Polish Airways."

I think Krakau (spelled "Cracow" in Polish and "Krakau" in German) was my favorite city. It is Poland's second largest city after Warsaw, and was Poland's capital until the sixteenth century. It was the only major city that was not reduced to rubble during World War II, so it retains its vast complex of old buildings of historical and architectural interest—the largest number of such in Poland (over one thousand), and has one of the largest old market squares in all of Europe. This Main Market Place retains its fourteenth century, real cobblestone pavement; its Old Cloth Hall, with its arcaded walk with souvenir shops behind; St. Mary's Church, with its two different-sized towers, out of which the tallest one has a trumpeter sounding a bugle call on the hour every hour night and day and which is broadcast all over Poland. (The story goes that a trumpeter sounded a warning call from this tower back in the early centuries to warn Krakau of a Tartar attack, and a Tartar arrow pierced his throat and killed him. So this continuing trumpet calling is in honor of this Krakau hero.) This church also contains a five-hundred-year-old wooden carved triptych altar piece, covered with gold, and made by Wit Stwosz. In the Cloth Hall, behind the first outside tier of shops, is an enclosed hall of souvenir shops, one right after another on both sides up and down the long hall.

We had one afternoon here to shop, but it was cold and rainy that day, and after buying a few things, we stood in line with some Poles and awaited our turn for a taxi to go back to our hotel. This was the only day it rained on us during the trip—naturally, it would rain on the only free afternoon we had to look around on our own and to shop!

One enterprising Polish woman amused us all. She had packaged up ten hand-colored wooden Easter eggs in separate plastic bags to sell to the tour bus people. We first met her outside our bus at the hotel, but seemingly she did such good business there that somehow she always managed to be, from then on, at every place our bus stopped with her huge bag of smaller plastic bags of eggs. The last I remember seeing her was on a corner near the Market Square where our bus had parked. She was waiting in the rain for the shoppers to return to the bus.

The last night at Krakau, we went to a fine restaurant to have a special fine meal, complete with white wine and vodka (those of us who didn't drink alcohol got watered-down orange juice instead), and a folk music performance by Poles dressed in native costumes. It was at this dinner that our Polish guide gave each of us ladies a hand-crafted doll dressed in the native costume of Krakau. (Since Jane and I were together, he gave me a girl and Jane a boy.) He gave each of the men a hand-carved wooden box about the size of a tobacco box. All were exceptionally nice gifts. (We would have felt cheated in just having had orange juice for our special drink, except we knew that orange juice is scarcer than either wine or vodka in Poland, so it was supposed to have been a special treat.)

The next morning we left Krakau for that infamous World War II concentration camp—Auschwitz ("Oswiecin" in Polish)—where the Nazis exterminated four million men, women, and children from twenty-nine different countries. It has been preserved and/or restored pretty much as it was in World War II. Auschwitz is about forty miles west of Krakau. It actually comprises about five different camps in this area, rich in iron and coal, where factory work could be carried on, as was done by these people brought here by the Nazis. Auschwitz's Birkenau was the main camp or headquarters, and that was the place we visited.

Behind its high barbed-wire walls were rows of mostly identical red brick buildings on either side of a dirt street. These were used to house these unfortunate people. (We were told that most of the people were gassed upon arrival—the old, the impaired, and the children, etc.—only the physically best of the people were kept for doing the work.) These buildings were mostly two stories high with a high-ceilinged basement under-floor, which necessitated one to walk up a flight of from six to eight well-worn outside steps to get to the first floor. Inside were rows of rooms on either side of an about eight-foot-wide hall. A lot of these rooms had been fronted with plate glass panels so today's visitors could see into these now bin-like structures in which had been piles (left dusty and worn as they originally were) of those grim reminders of man's inhumanity to man. One bin held shoes; others held clothing; some held luggage and bags of all types, while others were full of eye glasses, and one of the most horrible to view (bringing tears to many eyes) were those room-bins filled with little children's clothing and shoes.

In one of the buildings, these glass-fronted room-bins held human hair, shaved from the victims' heads as they had arrived. The Nazis had sorted the hair by color: one bin held only white hair, another blonde, others brown, red, and black. This was because the hair was to be woven into cloth and edgings and the like, and was to be shipped to Germany for this purpose. On display were some of the cloth and laces made from the hair.

Some of the rooms held the cans used to ship the ashes of the cremated people to Germany, where it was used for fertilizer. Each can held the remains of fifteen hundred victims. The cans didn't look that large, less than the size of a five-gallon lard can. The crematory building was a cement structure, not too far from the main gate where we entered. We had to go down a few steps to the underground interior, where the semicircular brick oven was at one end of a long passageway of a railroad leading right up to the open oven face. Here the corpses could be brought in on flat cars to be dumped into the oven and burned to ashes. The gas chambers were not too far distant.

One of the buildings was left so as to show how the people had lived. There were the sleeping rooms with their six-foot-long and about six-inch-deep old brown straw mattresses laid end to end and side by side on the cement floor. Here, also, were some bunk beds, looking much like old wooden stands where we stored potatoes in our cellar when we were kids at home. In another room were rows of out-in-the-open, unlidded toilets, in front of which were other rows of wash lavatories. There was at least one tall porcelain-tile stove in each building (stoves like used in old-time Germany).

There was a fifteen-foot space (approximately) between the buildings, and at the back of one of these up against a wall was where they made the Jews (and others) stand when they shot them down. There were several other busloads of visitors at Auschwitz the day we were there, and different ones had placed fresh-flower sprays and wreaths at the bottom of this wall. It was a sobering experience to see all those flowers lined up against that wall, knowing why they were there.

It was a cold, windy day—we had on coats or jackets, scarves or hats, and gloves, and were still chilly. This made us think of those poor Nazi prisoners, who had to stand outside for daily roll calls dressed only in thin clothing and without the benefit of coats. We were standing on the same soil, and we could almost feel their shivering, and hear their feet stomping in their attempt to keep warm. We were told that if someone was missing for roll call, the others had to stand there until the missing person was accounted for. So as to avoid standing there so long in the cold, they learned to drag out any who had died during the night, even if stiff, and stand them up in line.

Of course, most of the people held and exterminated here were Jews. And while we were there that day, an Israeli TV crew was there filming certain segments of this horror camp. We had to walk around one fellow who, with his camera on his shoulder, was filming, up close, one room of left-behind shoes.

Leaving Auschwitz, we drove to the border city of Cieszyn, part of which is in Czechoslovakia. Here we had our last lunch together at the Orbis Motel there. Jane and I waved good-bye to the rest of the bus people; and Teddy, our Polish guide, saw them across customs at the border. They would stay overnight in Czechoslovakia, take a sightseeing tour of Prague the next morning, and then head out for West Germany and home. We learned later that they rode all night again, getting into Germany on Easter Sunday morning, while we got there about two thirty Saturday afternoon.

Teddy got us a taxi, and we all three rode to the city of Katowice, the capital of Upper Selesia, where Teddy got us first-class train tickets for Warsaw. He told us the conductor told him the train was filled up, so Teddy bribed him with a few dollars to ensure us a first-class compartment. (This would be another long night ride, but not as long as that first night's train ride we had had.) Teddy carried our heavier suitcase, bought us some orange pop and ice cream, and got us in a first-class compartment for Warsaw. There was a very nice Polish couple in the compartment with us three. He could speak fluent English, as he was the English translator for a big Polish technical company. We enjoyed talking with him, but we all fell asleep sometime in the night, and when we awoke, it was about time to get off at Warsaw (around 11:00 p.m.), but we had had a long, long day. It was lightly sprinkling, and there was a long line awaiting taxis, so Teddy got us a private car, moonlighting as a taxi, and we were taken to the same hotel we had stayed in before, the Forum Hotel.

Teddy lived in Warsaw, so he told us he would be out the next morning to take us out to the airport in his own car. We had to leave on the plane around eight thirty; Teddy said he'd be at the hotel at 6:00 a.m. At a quarter of six our room phone rang, and there was Teddy. He had had the room service prepare us a breakfast, which was awaiting us at a coffee table in the hotel lobby, as the regular breakfast room wasn't open as yet. He had ordered sliced ham and cheese with hard rolls, coffee, and orange juice! I didn't want my orange juice, so I gave it to Teddy, knowing that he didn't get orange juice too often.

Since it was against their law for anyone to take out any of their paper money, one of the women on the bus had given Jane a five thousand zyloty bill rather than turn it over to the authorities at the Czech border, and Jane had around three thousand zyloty left. This we gave to Teddy rather than turning it over to the Communists at customs. (At the tourist rate of two thousand zyloty to the dollar, this would only amount to around four or five dollars; and we figured it was worth that, and more, for all Teddy had done for us, for he had acted as our own private guide. Of course, we had paid for our taxi and train ride to Warsaw, which was around fifteen dollars for the two of us, which was cheap.)

Teddy went with us at the airport as far as he was allowed and then waited to see if we got through customs okay. Naturally, we were apprehensive about going through customs, but at customs they just took our money declaration form, stamped it, and never asked us a thing. Relieved, we waved to Teddy and were on our way. It was easier getting out of Poland than it was getting in!

Teddy's real name was something like "Tadeusz"—a name hard to pronounce, so he told us all to just call him "Teddy." He was with the tour group from the time they crossed over the border from East Germany until they again crossed over into Czechoslovakia. Teddy was probably the best tour guide we have ever had in any country we have ever been in. It wasn't hard to understand him, as he could speak English well. He was friendly and congenial and fitted in so well with our group that we tended to think of him as an American rather than a Pole.

We had local guides at each one of the big cities—Gdansk, Warsaw, and Krakau—to tell us about their particular city. These were all women. The one at Gdansk couldn't speak English very well, but what she did say made us think that she might be a Communist. The one at Krakau was a professor of history at the university there.

Besides these, we had along the German tour guide, who was with the bus all the way from Germany and back again. She was an older woman, who had made many tours into these Eastern European countries for Scheffler Tours and could speak English fluently. Then there were two youngish German fellows who took turns driving that big tour bus. They were both excellent drivers and were both nice fellows.

Now that I have been inside Poland and safely out again, I think I would like to go back there someday to shop, but this time with the tourist rate exchange of two or three thousand zylotys to our dollar rather than the six hundred that we got as the official rate.

Yours for a free Poland,
love, Thelma

LESSON NO. 7

OUR DESIRES AND GOD'S ANSWERS

God is not against our traveling and doing things that are fun (if it's not something that is wrong). But I was having a terrible time finding a travel destination. It was, after all, my Easter vacation, and I longed to get away—needed to get away, in fact. But nothing was working out, and I found it to be very frustrating. It seemed that there was some problem associated with every place I thought of to visit.

And even though I was praying about which place to visit, my real desire was to go to Poland. God knew this, and had everything already planned out for us, even though we didn't realize this at first. He does, after all, give us the desires of our hearts (Psalm 37:4).

Later, after having visited Poland, we realized that we could not possibly have navigated on our own through this beautiful country, and therefore God kept us from going on our own and eventually worked out something much better for us.

This, then, is important to remember: God will work out the answer to our problems or our desires, but in His own way. We often have some idea about the solution to our problems, but God doesn't work according to our ideas. He has a better way of meeting our needs or our desires than we can ever imagine. We also need to realize that God answers our prayers in His own time. Many times we want the answer immediately, but this isn't how God operates. However, we know that even if God answers our prayer at the last minute, He always answers on time.

We may ask what our responsibility is in getting answers to our prayers. First, we have to pray according to God's will. We can't ask for something wrong (someone else's husband or wife, for instance). Second, we must believe that God answers prayer. And third, we must then do what we can to get the answer to our prayer. For instance, if praying about losing weight, we need to count the calories we devour at each meal and may also need to do some sort of exercise. God doesn't always do everything for us: we also have a part to play.

Thus I learned from this trip, and many others through the years, the secret of getting prayers answered. One needs to pray with faith, wait with patience, and work with diligence, for doing what we can to help ourselves shows faith.

CHAPTER 7

HEADHUNTERS, ASTRONAUTS, AND OTHER INTERESTING PEOPLE

One fall, on a missionary tour to the Far East, we happened to be in Taiwan at the time the granddaughter of a former headhunter was to be married, and we were privileged to be invited to the wedding. The wedding itself was similar to most here in the States, with the exception of the ceremony, which was all in Chinese, and also the unusual and colorful array of clothing we saw on the tribal people down from the mountains.

The most interesting part of this whole event, however, was the story the grandfather told. He was born and reared in a mountain area of Taiwan to parents who happened to be headhunters. One day he met some Christian missionaries who explained to him about Jesus and the way of salvation, and he gave his heart and life to the Lord. But when his parents found out about his decision, they kicked him out of their home.

However, later, upon hearing that his mother had become very sick, and knowing that the Christian missionaries could help her, this newborn child of God trudged up the mountain and literally carried his mother on his back all the way down to where the missionaries had a clinic. His mother was cured, and she and her whole family gave their hearts and lives to God. And now these family members, instead of being headhunters, are members of an evangelical church.

We were privileged to meet another interesting person while standing one morning in a line to get breakfast in the hotel where the "Full Gospel Businessmen's Fellowship" Convention was being held. My dad, who was always friendly and affable, started talking to the couple in line behind us. We learned that their names were Dottie and Charlie Duke, and that he had at one time been stationed on an air force base in Ramstein, Germany.

We later heard Charlie Duke speak at the convention and found out that he not only was an astronaut, but he had also been one of those who had walked on the moon. What impressed us the most, though, was hearing him say, "My walk on the moon was an experience of a lifetime, but it doesn't even begin to compare to my walk with Jesus Christ."

What a privilege it was to meet these two different people—a headhunter and an astronaut, but I've found in the course of traveling that there are many interesting people out there with exciting stories to tell. For instance, once on a trip to Spain my mom and I met a very unusual couple—a father and daughter who were from the United States. Let me relate the story as it happened.

My mom and I were trying to catch a train from Algerciras, Spain, to Granada, from where we would be flying back to Germany. Mom boarded the train (with all our luggage) in order to have a good seat for the long six-and-a-half-hour trip back while I went to get our tickets. As she was sitting there waiting for me, an older man in a sailor cap and jacket came by and said to her, "My daughter is with your daughter standing in a long, long ticket line. This train leaves at eleven thirty, and they are not going to make it by then." My mom started to get up and leave the train, saying to the man, "I have no money with me." (She had visions of the conductor, seeing that she had no ticket and no money with which to buy a ticket, dropping her off somewhere in this desert-like area of Spain.) The man hurriedly added, "But they intend to run and jump on the train without any tickets if the train starts to take off before they get them."

And this is exactly what happened. Karen and I left the long line and boarded the train just before it departed from the station. (We were later able to purchase tickets from the conductor.)

As we sat together with Karen and her father, Bill, we learned something about these two. They had crossed the Atlantic Ocean—just the two of them—in Bill's boat. During the fifty days it took to cross the ocean, they had had many strange experiences. For instance, one night a whale scared a swarm of squid, which tried to jump over their boat, but instead landed on it. So the next morning they had squid for breakfast. Once during the trip they ran out of bread and so popped corn to substitute for it.

Karen had had to stand watch at the ship's helm just like her dad, and one night during an Atlantic storm she and her bunk bed got so wet with saltwater that she and it never dried out, and she had to sleep in a very wet bed.

They had their boat anchored at the Algeciras Marina, living on it at night and then taking train and car trips all over Europe. But Karen declared she was not going to return to the States via her dad's boat. She thought it would be much better to fly over the ocean!

Having a bad experience can sometimes lead to making new acquaintances. My mom and I had just enjoyed a delicious lunch in our favorite little tea shop in Saverne, France, when I noticed, after getting in the car, a bumping sound on the left rear tire. I knew what it was—a flat tire—but I didn't know what to do about it, as my car manual was printed in German, and I couldn't read technical terms "auf deutsch" (in German). I pulled up to the curb just as a couple was passing by. The lady, speaking in English, said to me that her husband, unfortunately, was unable to help, but she would see if she could find a young man who could. After a short time she returned with a young man in tow who promptly began working on the tire.

Before long another young man, driving by and noticing our armed forces tags, also stopped to help, whereupon the French lady we now knew as Denise remarked, "I prayed for one angel, and God sent two." The two men soon had the flat tire off and the temporary on, and our new friends, Denise and Paul, hopped into the backseat in order to show us a place where we could get the tire repaired.

As we drove toward the tire shop, we learned more about Paul and Denise. She had been a teacher of English in a French high school, and Paul had been a career soldier. Now retired, they were enjoying their leisure time but also were enjoying attending "Full Gospel Businessmen's Fellowship" meetings. They were Catholics, but born-again and Spirit-filled. Needless to say, this was the beginning of a long friendship.

Another unusual mode of making acquaintances happened one summer when my mom and I were traveling around Czechoslovakia. Seeing some ladies in a newly mown field raking hay and piling it in large stacks, I stopped to take a picture. I had no sooner gotten back into my car, when one of the ladies appeared at the car window. She sounded rather gruff as she spoke. I didn't understand what she was saying, but I supposed she was telling me I needed to pay for taking their picture. I fumbled in my coin purse and came up with a handful of change, which I handed to her. But this was not what she wanted. Then after several minutes of straining to make herself understood, she handed me a piece of paper with her name and address on it. Finally, I understood—she wanted me to send her a postcard when I got back home.

So when we got back to Germany, we did send Marta, our new Czech friend, a postcard. But our correspondence didn't end there. For Christmas we sent Marta and her family a box of typical American-type goodies: chewing gum, popcorn, candy bars, peanut butter, etc. And she, in turn, sent us several Czech-made doilies for our furniture. One of Marta's daughters was learning English, and she did all the letter writing for the family. And thus for several years we corresponded.

These are some of the people I've met whose names I know, but there have been countless numbers of people who have been friendly and helpful whose names I never found out. The first weekend I was in Germany, for instance, I wanted to attend a church service where David Wilkerson was speaking. My roommates, who had already lived in Germany for a year, made a reservation for me in a hotel and saw that I got on the right train.

However, after I got off the train in Frankfurt and tried to get a taxi to take me to my hotel, I had problems. Every time a taxi pulled up, someone else jumped into it before I had a chance to even say a word. About the time I was ready to give up, a man came up to me and asked if I wanted a cab. He then proceeded to get the next one that drove up and helped me get in the backseat. Once seated, I turned to thank him, but he was nowhere to be seen. I've often wondered if he was an angel.

There are others without whose help we might have ended up in a bad way. When my mom and I were in Russia, our tour group, while following our guide, went on the longest and highest escalator I have ever ridden. Going down to the subway below, the escalator had dark stairs, the edges of which were unmarked, thus making it difficult for handicapped people. My mom had a vision problem, and when she stepped onto the escalator at the top, she fell. I stood yet at the top of the stairs, yelling in English, "Someone help my mom." I doubt anyone understood a word I said, but a man on the steps down below, seeing a body hurtling toward him, grabbed my mom's arm and lifted her up, holding on tightly to her until they reached the floor below.

Another time my mom had a fall was when we were at the beach into Deauville, France. Mom had been busy gathering shells and had her hands and arms full, when she suddenly stumbled over a boardwalk partially buried in the sand. The shells flew everywhere. However, the kindly French people came running from all directions, some helping my mom to her feet, and some even picking up the shells that she had dropped.

Another story from France involved me. Arriving by train in the city of Carcasonne, I immediately walked across the street from the train station to the first hotel I saw. However, they had no vacancies, but they did tell me that there was another hotel five minutes away. So I headed out. Walking along the street with a quick gait, I had passed by a park and had managed to get four or five blocks away but had not seen another hotel. I finally asked a lady where this particular hotel was, and she walked back with me, several blocks, so she could point out the hotel that I had missed, which was just around the corner from the first hotel!

Several times when traveling around Europe, I had people offer to help me carry a piece of luggage when I had several heavy pieces. So one time in France, I decided to return the favor. Seeing an elderly lady carrying a large, heavy suitcase, I volunteered to carry it for her to her room in the hotel where we were both staying. She couldn't seem to thank me enough, and the next day when I spotted the elderly lady and her daughter in a small café, they both began talking to me at the same time, no doubt thanking me again. But since they were both talking at the same time, I really didn't understand a word they said!

Once while visiting San Francisco, I wanted to see Chinatown, but had no idea how to get there. Passing a young man on the sidewalk, I asked him the directions for Chinatown. He said it would be easier for me to just follow him in his car than for him to tell me the way there. So we started out, the young man ahead with me following behind him, and when I would get hung up behind a red light, he would pull over to the curb and wait for me. Up and down the hill we went until we finally reached Chinatown. Once there, he waved good-bye to me, and I then enjoyed wandering around in this area. But I never forgot the help a total stranger had given to me.

LESSON NO. 8

PEOPLE ARE IMPORTANT

Each person is important to God—so important that if that person had been the only person on earth, Jesus would have died just for him or her. And God is interested in each person from conception to death.

But God, being a perfect gentleman, does not impose Himself upon anyone. By that I mean, He will convict and speak to each person individually, but He doesn't hound anyone. The Bible says, "The grace of God that bringeth salvation hath appeared to all men" (Titus 2:11). So we know from this verse that God speaks to each and every individual. And, therefore, no one can give the excuse that they never heard the gospel. Helen Keller, who was born both blind and deaf, was taught one day by her teacher the word for "God." And she said something like this, "I'm so glad you told me His name, for He has spoken to me many times." From this we can deduce that there is no one to whom God has not spoken.

We also know that God has a life's plan for each individual, and finding that plan will give great contentment. The Bible says in Jeremiah 1:5, "Before I formed thee in the belly, I knew thee." In other words, He knew what we would be like and what we would do in life before we were even born. And, therefore, He has placed within us the gifts or assets we would need to carry out His plan in our lives.

Many times people never find their true calling in life, though, because they do not make God their Lord and Savior. And, on the other hand, some people find their calling, but because they have not made God their Lord, their life's calling is not used to better the world or to help others, but is used in a selfish sort of way.

Thus it's important for all people to give their hearts and lives to God for several important reasons: (1) their lives on earth become the best possible lives they could ever have, and (2) when they die they will go to heaven rather than to hell.

The lesson, then, that I learned from meeting and getting acquainted with the many different people I encountered in my travels taught me that there are all kinds of interesting, likable, and helpful people in this world. And it was my privilege to chance upon these very special people.

CHAPTER 8

GHOSTS, BUGS, AND STRANGE NIGHT EXPERIENCES

One spring when a friend and I were traveling in France we chanced upon an old chateau that had been made into a hotel. Deciding to spend the night there, we unpacked and got ready for bed. Before falling off to sleep, though, we had had a discussion about the chateau, which was by then in total darkness and seemed rather eerie. We had even joked about the ghosts that were probably lurking in the quiet, dark hallways.

Feeling rather chilly in the night, I remembered that Peggy had piled her bedspread, along with the lingerie she had exchanged for her nightgown, on an old bureau sitting over against one of the thick cement walls. Hurrying over, I grabbed the bedspread, threw it on my bed, and quickly hopped back under the covers.

Later in the night Peggy awoke. As she glanced down to the floor, she noticed something large and white lying there. Remembering our earlier conversation, she lay in bed and tried to figure out just what that puddle of white was. She knew it couldn't be light shining in through the windows, as there were no lights outside at all. She also knew that splash of white wasn't there when we went to bed.

Finally she could stand the suspense no longer and got up to investigate. Carefully groping her way in the dark, she cautiously reached down to touch the white puddle. At the first touch, she realized it was not a ghost, but rather her white slip, which I had accidentally dropped onto the floor when I had pulled the bedspread off the bureau!

I had a different experience one Easter vacation when I went to Spain. Being all night on the train, I was extremely tired when I arrived in Barcelona. Consequently, I booked a room in a pension at the train station, and then hurried by taxi out to the place I was to stay, anxious to hop into bed and make up for the sleep I had lost. When I pulled back the covers of the bed, however, a large cockroach went racing across the sheets. At that point I was too tired to care, and, crawling into bed, I promptly fell asleep.

The next morning was a different story, though, when I found more bugs crawling in the small sink in the room. One night of sleeping with bugs was about all I could take, and so I cut my vacation short and headed back to my apartment in Germany.

On another trip through France—this time by train—I decided to get off the train around midnight in a city called Lille rather than going on any farther, as I had earlier planned. Walking across the street from the train station, I spotted a hotel. The man at the desk was working, because of the late hour, as both clerk and porter.

While I was at the desk registering for the night, another guest came in—a man—and set his white suitcase down next to my white pieces. After I got registered, the clerk came around from behind his desk, picked up the man's white suitcase and then indicated for me to follow him. So I picked up my two white suitcases and went upstairs with the desk clerk in the lead. The clerk, now turned porter, then walked into a room carrying the other guest's suitcase.

I, in the meantime, waited out in the hall, as I thought he would show me my room next. This was not to be the case, though, as I heard the clerk telling me this was my room. Knowing a little about the French way of life, I became incensed that the clerk was putting me in the same room with a strange man. I tried to explain to the desk clerk that there was no way I would share my room with some man, but at midnight I could barely speak my own language, let alone French. Finally, though, I was able to get across to the clerk that the piece of luggage he had carried upstairs was not mine. The clerk, at finding out this bit of information, was quite embarrassed with the mistake he had made as it dawned on him that the piece of luggage he was holding belonged to the man downstairs. And the man downstairs—he was probably waiting and wondering just what had happened to his piece of luggage.

One of the strangest night experiences occurred while on a tour my mom and I had taken to the Middle East. At the beginning of the tour we had eaten at the same table several times with an elderly man and his wife. The man later came down with some "bug" and got extremely ill—so ill, in fact, he had to leave the tour and fly back home. Evidently, my mom and I caught the same bug, and while in Egypt, we became very sick. After spending several days in the hotel in bed, we were astonished to awaken one night and find a man right out of the pages of *A Thousand and One Nights* storybook standing at the foot of our beds. He had on a long silk robe and silk shoes with toes that turned up at the ends. It turned out that he was a doctor, and even though he looked like an Arabian prince, the medicine he gave us worked, and we were able to continue on with the tour.

A different and not so pleasant experience occurred while I was living in Italy. Coming back to my apartment late one evening, I noticed a number of cars parked on the street, all of which had American armed forces license plates (evidently my American neighbors in the apartment below me were having a party), and walking among the cars were three or four Italian men.

Because gas was so expensive in Europe (around five dollars a gallon), our American government bought up gas coupons at the going European price and sold them to us for a lesser price. Since many Americans kept their coupons in the glove compartment of their cars, I figured the men I saw walking among the cars were trying to find an unlocked car, so they could help themselves to "free" gas coupons.

As I stood at my bedroom window watching the men, one of them noticed me and started ringing my doorbell down by the front door of the building. Later, as one of the people at the party exited, the Italian man slipped into the building and came right up to my apartment, ringing my doorbell upstairs. I sat down on the floor in the dark feeling frightened as the man blocked my only way out of the building. I prayed, and finally the man left.

Several months later, a car filled with Italian men, no doubt the same ones who had come before, pulled up under my bedroom window. And when I looked down on them, they started throwing rocks at my window. Feeling the same fear as before, I again began to earnestly pray. Suddenly there was a loud clap of thunder, and all the lights in the parking lot went out! I then heard the Italian car screech out of the parking lot on two wheels—;no doubt the driver feeling eerily terrified. Fortunately, after this experience, this group never returned!

While most of my night experiences have not been frightening ones, some have been quite interesting. For instance, one night while traveling with my mom through Belgium, we spotted a sign by the highway advertising a hotel. Turning down the narrow highway, we found the hotel in the middle of a pasture. Entering the lobby, we noticed various saddles and bridles, some hanging on pegs on the walls and some lying on the floor. That evening when we went down to eat, we found one long table (rather than separate small tables) at which everyone staying in the hotel was sitting. Since we were given no menu, we all enjoyed the same food.

Our room, though not spectacular, was comfortable, clean, and quiet. However, early in the morning the quiet was broken by sounds of whinnying, snorting, and trotting. As we looked out the window we saw people in a pen at the back of the hotel riding around on horses. Evidently we had stumbled upon a hotel that was a type of riding school!

On another trip through Belgium, having found no hotel for the night, I inquired about places to stay at a filling station I had noticed at the edge of a town. The man working at the station could speak no English, but he told me, speaking only in French, about a very nice hotel located out in the country, and he then gave me the directions to it. He even called the hotel to tell them we were coming.

I started out heading down a very narrow and very dark road, getting farther and farther away from town. As we drove for miles and had found no hotel, I began to wonder if I had understood the man's French correctly. But all-of-a-sudden we came upon a large building with all of its outdoors lights on. The people at the hotel were expecting us! This hotel turned out to be an old mill that had been converted into an exceptionally beautiful and modern place to stay. Our room even had a small stream running under it, which helped to lull us to sleep that night.

One of the most intriguing experiences we've had, however, was on a trip we took in 1971 through Yugoslavia. Staying one night in a small town in what was known as the White Borderland (an area in Yugoslavia where the woman wore white native costumes) my mom, who was visiting over my Christmas vacation, and I stayed in a hotel room in what my mom called "the little hotel's presidential suite"—a room at the front of the building and right over the canopied entrance below.

On the main first floor was a dining room and bar where some of the townsmen had gathered this night and were singing what sounded like native folksongs which they sang most of the night. We crept down once to listen to them, but the moment they spotted us, they shut up. After we left, they started up again, keeping us awake most of the night.

Only getting to sleep toward morning, my mom was suddenly awakened with the words spoken in German, "Glory to God in the highest, alleluia." Listening intently for anything further, my mom heard nothing more except for the click-clacking of horses' hooves outside, which faded into the distance. This was certainly an unusual way to be awakened, and especially in a Communist country!

As we drove along that day we tried to figure out just what this strange night message might have meant. The one conclusion we came to was that it couldn't have been any of the native people, as they spoke no German. And since it was an early Sunday morning, and very few people were out and about, we began to doubt that it was a human being at all. But was it an angel? We never did find out.

Some night experiences have been different and even a bit frustrating. Late one night in California we spied from the freeway a motel that had a vacancy sign. But finding the right exit to the motel in the dark proved to be a challenge. I drove miles before coming to an exit that, unfortunately, turned out to be the wrong one to the motel, and then I drove even more miles to get back on the freeway. This happened three times before I ever found the right exit, and when I at last got to the motel, the motel sign said, "No vacancies," as it was now after midnight. I inquired about a room anyway and found the manager had one unit left that he would rent. It was a large unit with four bedrooms and several bathrooms. So after all our problems in getting to the motel, we were thrilled to be able to luxuriate in our own separate bedroom and bath!

Many times in my travels around Europe I spent the night sitting up on a hard, cold train seat that was covered in stiff plastic material. I found I could actually sleep fairly well on trains as their swaying motion tended to lull me to sleep. Most of the European trains at this time had glassed-in compartments with seating for six people on one side of the train and a very narrow passageway on the other side.

One year at Easter the trains were so crowded that I could not find a single seat in any of the compartments. Consequently, I had to pull down a small fold-up seat from the wall out in the passageway. And that's where I spent the night. Once in the night, however, I woke to discover a fellow passenger sitting next to me—a young Italian man—sound asleep with his head lying on my shoulder!

Several times my mom's and my motel room turned out to be the front seat of our car. Traveling one summer to the Grand Canyon, we found once we got there that there were no rooms available. This was because a film company was making a movie, *Brighty of the Grand Canyon*, and all the rooms then available at the Grand Canyon were rented. Since it was so far to drive back to the next nearest town, we just curled up in the front seat of the car and went to sleep. But we received a very special bonus in the process. As the sun rose over the canyon early in the morning, we hopped out of the car, and, walking over to the canyon's edge, we drank in the awe-inspiring colors as they changed from pale lavender and blue to brilliant colors of red and orange.

LESSON NO. 9

IN THE DARK OF THE NIGHT

While the nighttime may represent rest, it can also be a synonym for terror, anguish, or worries. We know from various scripture verses that darkness and night can be a time of evil or of sorrow; for the Bible says, "Weeping may endure for the night, but joy cometh in the morning" (Psalm 30:5). Therefore, we see that while nighttime may represent sorrow, daylight represents joy.

It's in the middle of the night that robbers prowl about when they can't be seen so well. And it's in the nighttime of a person's life that the devil makes his appearance, bringing all kinds of anguish and problems. Many times these problems can be so overwhelming that a person doesn't know which way to turn. For instance, in the quiet of the night when a person feels all alone, the diagnosis of cancer can be frightening. Or it's in the night that a person may become consumed with financial worries.

Once when I was going through a particularly trying time, I heard this statement in a dream: "There's light at the end of the night." In other words, the night does eventually end, and with it, the problem also. And since God is always there patiently waiting (in fact, he never sleeps—Psalm 121:4), we can know that He's waiting and willing to help us. We just need to turn our problems over to him.

One of the important stories in the Bible is that of the children of Israel coming up to the Red Sea and being able to walk across on dry land. The reason for their being able to do this is that God worked all through the night to drive the waters back. And this is what He does when we have a period of darkness in our lives too.

However, while God can help us with terrifying problems, the worst darkness perhaps is the darkness of one's heart. Without

God living in our life, our "heart is desperately wicked" (Jeremiah 17:6). And this wickedness carries over into everything a person does. While a person may seem good outwardly, inwardly there may be much turmoil and grief. Therefore, it's important to have our hearts cleansed by the precious blood of Jesus, because the darkness will not go away by any other means. We just need to ask Jesus to forgive our sins and to come into our hearts and lives. And He will do just that.

CHAPTER 9

ACTIVATING THE TASTE BUDS

E ating out in nice restaurants has always been a special joy to me, but sometimes figuring out just what I had eaten has been a challenge. Not knowing the language when I first went to Germany, I figured the best way to order a meal in a restaurant was by the "point and guess" method. Once after ordering an entrée called "Kalbsnierenbraten," I later looked up the word in my German-English dictionary and found I had eaten fried calf kidneys. Now the idea of eating kidneys did not much appeal to me, so I always avoided that particular meal when I ate out in Germany.

However, one Thanksgiving I traveled by train to Zermatt, Switzerland, a French-speaking region. This time the menu in the restaurant in which I ate my Thanksgiving meal was in French. My "point and guess" method proved to be just as hazardous as when I ate in Germany for I had once again ordered fried kidneys—only this time in French!

Shortly after I first arrived in Germany, the principal of the small school where I was teaching took all four of us teachers out to a typical Bavarian restaurant for an evening meal. (Bavaria was the state in which our school was located.) We had an especially good meal, but the dessert was superb. I never forgot the name of it—"Konigs Kuchen" (kings cake). So when I found it listed on a menu in a restaurant in Coburg I told my mom, who was visiting me at the time, "We must have this dessert." This was a soufflé-type of cake that came as a large, hot dish that needed to be baked after it was ordered.

We didn't realize however, it would take so long for it to appear on our table. And so we waited and waited. Finally, though, the waiter brought out a big bowl piled high with foamy white stuff covered with red syrup and two plates on which to put it. "This doesn't look like the desert as I remember it," I told my mom as I ladled it out onto the two plates. (I had never found it in any restaurant since that first time of experiencing it.) My mom started eating hers, and remarked to me, "This tastes just like whipped cream with raspberry syrup on it." To which I replied, "No, Mother, this has to be that dessert, as they're not bringing any other. Let's just go ahead and eat it." So we both proceeded to eat the white foamy stuff covered with raspberry syrup.

Quite a while later the waiter came bearing a huge platter of hot baked meringue-covered dessert. He looked rather odd at us when he noticed the topping had all been eaten but never said a word! And the two of us—we couldn't eat even half of the dessert after having had such a large meal of pork and then a big bowl of whipped cream!

One Veteran's Day weekend a friend and I decided to spend our holiday in France. At that time I lived only fourteen miles from the French border and always enjoyed driving over there. We had planned to do sightseeing, but since it rained the entire weekend, and we didn't particularly enjoy sightseeing in the rain, we thought we would, instead, spend our time eating lunch and dinner in Michelin-starred restaurants. Restaurants in France, especially the nice ones, are rated by stars, three stars being the very best. And eating in France, and especially at a starred restaurant, is tantamount to the best sightseeing one could ever do.

Enjoying a meal in France is not a hurried affair, either. First, it takes awhile for the food to come. And, second, most of the meals consist of three or four courses. So to eat two meals a day in France can take up most of the day. Consequently, this was a holiday in which we ate our way through one corner of France.

One of my favorite European restaurants was a small one in Venice, Italy with the unsophisticated name of Harry's Bar, a restaurant made famous by Ernest Hemingway. Having a unique atmosphere, this restaurant, with an unprepossessing decor, has a dining area with small round tables situated so close together that the guests can literally rub elbows with one another.

In this restaurant, which boasts of having the smallest kitchen in the world, one can experience the best of Italian cooking. One of my favorite dishes was "tagliatelle verde," or green noodle casserole. But in the fall, shortly after the grapes have been picked, a glass of freshly squeezed grape juice, skin and all, was one of the most delectable drinks I've ever had, and was another favorite from this restaurant.

And speaking of drinks, most of the water around the world is not safe to drink. Consequently, the native people have found other substitutes—coffee, tea, beer, wine, bottled water, etc. Once in a German Gasthaus a friend and I ordered some tea. However, some German men seated at a table across from ours evidently thought we needed something more invigorating, so they had the waitress bring us a small glass of liqueur. Since we were both teetotalers, we ignored the liquor. Evidently, the men thought we didn't like this drink, so they ordered us another kind, this one supposedly sweeter than the first. Not wanting to offend the men, we poured the second drink into our teapot when they weren't looking and hoped they would not be so kind as to order us anymore!

Various restaurants around the world can be quite interesting, not only for their cuisine and décor, but also for their patrons. For instance, while vacationing one Christmas in Monaco, my mom and I ducked into a restaurant to eat and to also get out of the rain. Other people also wandered in to get out of the rain. The thing we noticed, though, was that about every person had a dog on a leash along with him or her. It seemed as though there were as many dogs in the café as there were people. Some of the dogs even sat on the chairs at the tables. Of course, the waiters, to be polite, had to speak to each dog as well as its person. And all of the dogs, because it was so cold outside, wore knitted coats. But to top it all off, the dogs were so well behaved that there was not a single dog fight!

Eating at home in my German or Italian apartments could prove to be a challenge at times. Since my American appliances did not fit in either German or Italian outlets, and because the electric current was also different, it was necessary to buy a transformer to use for toasters, mixers, etc. One morning while getting ready for school, I plugged the toaster into the transformer, but when I plugged the transformer into the wall outlet, "pop!" went the fuse. This necessitated my going down six flights of stairs to the basement to flip the switch. When I got back upstairs I again replugged everything, only to have the transformer go out again. After several times of this happening I was no longer in the mood for toast, or anything else, for that matter. The only good thing about that morning was that I had gotten my daily exercise!

Small food shops in Europe are quite different from those we have in the States. There are supermarkets, but the little specialty shops are the most common— that is, meat shops, bakeries, cheese stores, etc. When shopping, I found it was important to know, not only the names of various foods, but to also know the weights. For instance, I once ordered in a pastry shop a kilo of hors d'oeuvres—little pizzas and other meat-type pastries. Having no idea how much a kilo of small pastries would be, I was shocked, not only when I saw the huge box they came in, but also at the price!

It was an experience, though, just to walk along and look in the shop windows. Once in Breccia, Italy, we noticed, in a meat market, pans of small birds—feathers off, but with their feet and legs still on. They looked just like sparrows and probably were, as we saw very few sparrows hopping around on the Italian streets. There was also a brace of thrush-like birds—heads and feathers still on—hanging up in their windows, as well as a few feathered pigeons in among the other meat.

Besides all these birds, they had a whole pan of red rooster combs for sale for cooking and eating. (I once had a rooster comb in my meal at a French restaurant, and I can't say I found it particularly tasty.) Other meats they had displayed were huge snails and octopuses. Hanging up, lining the walls inside the meat market, were big furry rabbits with heads and legs still on.

This market wasn't nearly as bad as an open-air market I once chanced upon in Tunisia. Dangling from the ceiling were camel's and cow's heads complete with thousands of flies!

But getting back to our Italian city—the pastry shops at this time of year had long hunks of black cake, the tops of which were covered with powdered sugar. They called it "Pana Morti" or "Bread of Death." It was baked for "All Soul's Day," which was in this particular year on November 5. It looked quite good, so we bought some to eat. They sold it by the kilo, and the piece we got cost over a dollar. It tasted like chocolate fruitcake—candied lemon peel and nuts were in it—and it was also heavy like a fruitcake. At the price of it, I allowed that the Italian people just ate a thin slice of it now and then for dessert and didn't gulp it down in hunks as we did!

Eating in various places around the world has left some lasting impressions. For instance, my mom, in a letter telling about food in the Normandy area of France, said that she loved the sole fish that we got in that area. This was one of their specialties. But it bothered her that it was quite often served with an eight- to ten-inch shrimp complete with shell, feelers, and legs all wound in a circle decorating the top of the fish. She didn't much appreciate two black eyes staring up at her!

And I'll never forget the piece of apple pie I once ordered in a restaurant in England. The waitress asked if I wanted cream on it, and I, thinking she meant ice cream, said, "yes." However, when she returned, she had a small pitcher of thick cream which she slowly poured over my apple pie!

On a trip to South America, while visiting in the home of a native of Ecuador, our tour group watched a group of guinea pigs frolicking around on the floor. Only a few days later, however, we were given a whole baked guinea pig at a restaurant in which we were eating. I couldn't help but remember, though, the day we had watched the playful animals, and I felt as though I was eating someone's pet.

Not all food experiences have been strange ones, though. To this day I can still remember and relish in my mind some of the different and delicious foods I have had. For instance, in a German restaurant one particular meal on the menu came with a small edible basket made of potatoes and filled with vegetables. Nor will I ever forget a cave-like restaurant in a small German town that served crunchy potato balls covered with nuts and deep-fat fried. They were scrumptious! And once in a restaurant in Yugoslavia, we were given a large round loaf of rye bread to eat with our meal. I've never before had bread that tasted so much like cake.

After having lived in Europe for twenty-five years, it was my last day before returning to the States permanently. I walked downtown on a gorgeous June day in order to enjoy one last ice cream sundae at an Italian café. This particular sundae was called "spaghetti ice." The vanilla ice cream was squeezed through a ricer, which caused the ice cream to come out looking like long pieces of spaghetti. Strawberry syrup was put on top of the spaghetti-looking ice cream, which was then covered with ground-up nuts. This made the sundae now look like it had tomato sauce with Parmesan cheese on it. As I sat at an outdoor table, a soft, warm breeze was gently blowing, and across the street a young man was singing a soft melody accompanied by his guitar. What a memorable way to end my last day!

LET THE GOOD TIMES ROLL

Some of life's most memorable moments can take place around the dinner table. When friends and/or relatives sit down to enjoy a meal together, not only can the conversation be pleasant, but the taste buds may also get a real treat. We know from reading in the Bible that even Jesus had enjoyable moments eating with friends.

The lesson I learned, then, from enjoyable eating experiences is that God wants us to have good things in life. The Bible says in 3 John 1:1 that God's desire for us is "to prosper and be in health." In other words, He wants everything we do to work out well for us.

Sometimes things don't work out so well for us, though, and the cause may be one of these five reasons: (1) we have sinned, (2) a particular desire may not be God's will for us, (3) the devil may try to stop what God has for us, (4) sometimes it takes awhile for God to work out that particular desire, and (5) we don't have enough faith. It's our business, then, to figure out which of these five might be the reason for things not going so well. So let's examine each of these.

1. We have sinned. When we do wrong, our relationship to God is broken. The Bible says, "If I regard iniquity in my heart, the Lord will not hear me" (Psalm 66:18). Therefore, we need to repent for the wrong we've done, and if our wrongdoing involves someone else, we may need to make things right with the wronged individual.

2. This particular desire may not be God's will for us. I believe that God only says "yes" to us, for the Bible says, "For all the promises of God in Him are yea"

(2 Corinthians 1:20). However, if our desire is something that will cause us harm or heartache, God may say to us, "I have something better for you." We have to keep in mind that God is always positive, and, therefore, His answer isn't no, but is something so much better than we might be asking.

3. The devil may try to stop what God has for us. The devil is our number one enemy. He has no love for anyone, not even those who serve him. Therefore, he will try to bring harm to us whenever he can. And if the desire we have is to bring glory to God, the devil will work especially hard to keep this desire from fruition. Thus, we need to be especially prayerful if the devil is the cause of our not getting the answer to our prayer.

4. Sometimes it takes awhile for God to work out the answer to our desire. We don't always understand why our prayers are delayed or why we may have to wait so long for the answer. We know from biblical history, however, that impatience or doing our own thing never works out for our best. A good example of this is Abraham, who after having waited thirty years for the son promised by God to him and Sarah, took matters into his own hands and had a child by Hager, Sarah's maid. We know from current history that the result of this unpromised child has caused many problems for the Jewish people.

5. We don't have enough faith. We know that God requires us to have faith in order to get answers to our prayers, for the Bible states, "According to your faith, be it unto you" (Matthew 9:29). However, some problems in life are so severe (cancer, for instance) that faith for healing seems next to impossible. When we experience this kind of situation, there are several things we can do. First, we

may need to ask someone else to pray for us and with us. And second, we need to learn the lesson of praying clear through. By that, I mean praying until you feel God and know that He has said yes to your request.

When we learn, therefore, the reason for our unanswered prayer, we need to pray and then leave the results in God's hands, knowing He will work out that which is best for us.

CHAPTER 10

STORMING THE CASTLE AND OTHER FAUX PAS

From an antique shop in the city of Vaduz, Liechtenstein, I saw a sign that pointed to a castle. My mom and I, having arrived in this principality by train the night before, were ambling about the city streets. Thinking the castle might be interesting to visit, I suggested we walk up to the top of the street to see it. This street, however, was up the side of a mountain. It wound around and finally curved off to the right, but just kept going on and on upward. It seemed as if we walked miles, and it was damp and foggy out. To encourage my mom to keep going, I kept telling her the castle was just a bit farther or just around the curve. But we did eventually find it. And to our surprise we found ourselves on top of the mountain that was just back of our hotel!

When we reached the castle, we discovered we could not find any open entrances to visit it. So I began to pound on a huge, heavy iron door and tried to open it, but it was locked. The gate to the castle was also shut. We decided it was either the wrong time of the year for visitors or, as I observed, "There's a TV antenna; maybe someone lives in the castle." Finally we saw a gatekeeper walking away from the place, and I asked him if we could go in and visit the castle. He replied, "Nein" (or no). Thus we had that entire exhausting walk for nothing. We took a maple-leaf strewn path back down the mountainside. The path was wet and slippery, and its banks were lined with trees, bushes, ferns, and snails. It must have been beautiful in the springtime when the flowers would have been in bloom also.

I had given Mom a pair of my pantyhose to wear, but they were a little too small for her and so kept sliding down, particularly as we walked up and down hills, when her body would be at a wrong angle. She looked around; there was no one in sight, and it was still very foggy. So she pulled up her skirt and wiggled the pantyhose back into position. After she got the hose pulled up, she noticed her slip had gotten stuck around her waist. So again up with her skirt in order to pull back down her slip. I laughed and laughed at her predicament as I kept watch for cars or other walkers.

After we got down the mountainside to the town below, we decided to buy some picture postcards of the castle. And there on the backs of the cards was printed "Residence of the Ruling Prince." No wonder they wouldn't let us in to visit. Their monarch lived there! And we'd been pounding on his door trying to storm his castle!

Sometimes we've made mistakes because of not knowing either the rules of the culture we were in or the correct name for a particular thing. For instance, my mom and I both learned quickly what restrooms were called in Europe. At the airport in Rome, Mom asked at the information booth (where they could speak English) where the "restrooms" were. They actually had to call in someone to understand what it was she wanted. But from then on, she knew that "restrooms" in Europe were called "toilets."

Making mistakes in speaking another language is very easily done, however. One time my mom and I were driving along the

"Wine Route" in the Alsace region of France. We had stopped at an antique shop along the way, and I had told the owner of the shop that my mom had had an antique shop in the States. At least that is what I thought I had said. But later I realized that I had made a mistake in my French verbs, and I had, in reality, told the shop owner that my mom was an antique! But maybe at the age of eighty she really was.

Earlier my mom had made a mistake when a waitress, at a tea room where we many times would enjoy a drink and a pastry, asked her what she wanted to drink. I had gone to the restroom, and Mom was left alone to order. She told the waitress in French that we wanted "good-bye." The two words, "to drink" and "good-bye," sound quite a bit alike in French. But she learned from this mistake and never again used the wrong word for "drinks."

An embarrassing faux pas was made once on a train. Traveling all day through Italy, my mom and I decided to eat our lunch in the dining car. Since this particular car was somewhat crowded, we shared a table with an elderly Italian man and his son. Seeing a bottle of water on the table, my mom helped herself to a glassful. And the Italian man said to her as she poured the water from the bottle into her glass, "*Prego*" (please). Several times my mom helped herself to a drink. But eventually a waiter appeared and informed Mom that one had to buy bottles of water, and this particular bottle had been bought by the elderly Italian man. My poor mom was so embarrassed, but the kindly Italian gentleman just seemed to take this faux pas in his stride and continued to say "*Prego.*"

We had another Italian experience when my mom, who was visiting me, and I drove over to Trieste one Saturday. It was gently raining when we started out but turned into a real downpour before we got back home. However, even in a drizzle, it was a pretty drive as we looked down from our mountain highway upon the beautiful blue Adriatic Sea.

We finally came to a place in the road where there were some men in uniform and a hut-like shelter. I pulled off the road and said, "I think that we must have come to the Yugoslav border." The men immediately surrounded us, and when I asked one of them if this was the Yugoslav border, he called another man over and told him that we spoke Spanish! This last guy started babbling something to us and kept saying, "Passport." So we both pulled out our passports. Then he asked for my to "Trittico" card. He finally understood that we did not want to go into Yugoslavia but had just lost our way and had gotten on the wrong road. So he motioned for us to go up farther and turn around. I drove up and pulled off to the side to turn around and got stuck in the mud! For a while it looked as if we were going to be spending the night in Yugoslavia, whether we wanted to or not. It was quite dark by this time and just pouring down rain. We finally did get out of the mud, though, and got turned around and headed back to Trieste, being waved on as we passed the Italian customs. When we got back to Trieste, we walked around in the rain and looked in the shop windows with about half a million other people, (or so it seemed) being relieved that we were still in Italy!

I had a very unusual problem once on a trip to Germany. One Veteran's Day holiday a friend and I headed out for Munich, Germany. When we left, the weather in the Northern Italian town of Aviano, where we both taught, was typical fall weather—rainy and cloudy but with no snow. However, when we got to the Brenner Pass (the passageway in Austria through the Dolomite Mountains), it had become quite dark, and the highway was covered with snow and seemed rather slick. Stopping at a small restaurant to get a bite to eat, we asked the owner what the highway was like ahead, and he told us it was very bad. So we decided to not go on any farther, but to find a hotel in which to spend the night. Somehow as we were unpacking the car, I managed to leave my car keys in the ignition and then lock the door. Since it was so late, I didn't try to retrieve the keys. But I didn't sleep well that night for worrying about someone stealing my little "Bug." However, the next morning my car was still there, and with the aid of a clothes hanger I was able to unlock the car door, and we headed on our way

In the daylight the mountain pass was manageable, and we had no further problems until we reached Munich. Since it was nearing bedtime, we began to look for a place to spend the night. My friend wanted to stay in the Schwabing area, which was an artists' hangout. Thus we headed in that direction. We found many pensions (hotels), but none suited Dorothy, and so we kept looking.

Finally, though, I let her out to check another pension, and she came back to the car stating that this one was acceptable, and we could spend the night there. Since I needed to find a place to park my car overnight, I told Dorothy I would be back soon, and I headed out down the dark street. Streets in Germany are never in square blocks, and consequently, I had to drive several kilometers before I found a street I could turn on and come back to the pension.

Remembering that the pension was on a corner, and right across from it was a small grocery store, I parked the car and went into a building that looked like the one I had seen Dorothy enter. But when I went to the manager of the pension, she stated that not only was my friend not there, but no Americans were staying there at all.

Since there were many pensions along the street, I started to go to each and every one but found no Dorothy. It was nearing midnight, and I was getting concerned since I couldn't find my friend, and she had all our luggage. A young German couple exiting from one of the buildings noticed my despair and offered to help me look for her. So we continued on down the long block, asking in every pension, but with no luck. At the corner of the next street, a corner that was identical to the one I had just been on, I entered a pension, and there was Dorothy! I had just been looking a block too soon!

Not all strange experiences in Germany were mine, however. One fall my uncle flew over to Germany to spend some time with me while also visiting Europe. On weekends when I wasn't teaching I would take him to see some of the famous landmarks and interesting places nearby. But during the week he was on his own. Early one morning I put him on a train that was going to Freiburg, an interesting and unique town down in the Black Forest. I showed him where to get off when he returned and told him how many stops the train would make before getting back to Karlsruhe, where I would pick him up.

When I went after school to the train station to pick him up, however, he wasn't there. I waited for the next train, and still no Uncle Ivan. Frantic with worry, I went home and called my mom, who was in the States, as I had no idea where in the world he was, and I knew he didn't have much money with him, nor did he speak the German language. My mom and I prayed about the situation, and I went back once again to the train station. This time I found him! He had boarded a fast train out of Freiburg, and, consequently, the number of stops the train made was not the same number I had told him. Therefore, he went beyond Karlsruhe all the way up to Mannheim, a city some seventy miles from where he was to get off. Fortunately, when he noticed he was at the wrong city, he found a train going to Karlsruhe, and all ended well!

I may have committed a faux pas several times with my camera. Tagging along at the end of a line of people going up a narrow mountain path in Tunisia to visit a troglodyte home, I stopped once as we were nearing the cave home to take a picture of some animals in a small pen. At that moment a teenaged fellow ran up to me yelling, "No, no, you can't take a picture here." I didn't take a picture, but just to show me who was in charge, he gave me a hard push. And if I hadn't caught my balance, I would have tumbled down the side of the mountain!

Something similar happened on a trip I took once to India. While watching a parade, I thought I'd take a picture of some small boys—boys around nine or ten years of age—walking in the parade. However, I never took the picture, but one of the boys, thinking I had, came up to me and demanded some money. When I wouldn't give him any, he gave me a hard push, causing me to fall against another lady. Fortunately, I never fell clear to the pavement, which might have caused a serious problem. But such is the lot of women in Middle East countries!

LESSON NO. 11

TO ERR IS HUMAN

Everyone makes mistakes. And some mistakes can be quite serious: for instance, losing a large amount of invested money in a Ponzi scheme situation, or being the cause of a terrible accident that might cause someone their very life.

But what I found out in life is that there is nothing that God can't handle, even if it's a very serious problem. We just need to learn to put the bad situation in His hands, and let Him work it out.

However, there are certain lessons we need to learn in order to avoid bad situations. First of all, we should learn to conduct our business affairs and, indeed, everything we do in life, with wisdom. The Bible tells us that if we don't have wisdom, we can ask, and God will give it to us (James 1:5). And wisdom is different from intelligence. A person can be intelligent but not wise, because wisdom comes from God.

A second lesson we need to learn is to listen to the warnings God gives to us. Sometimes we may feel a prick in our spirit that we shouldn't continue on the way we're going. And this may be God giving us a warning. But God also warns through dreams. We see this happening many times in the Bible. In fact, God used dreams four times in connection with the life of Jesus.

Someone might then ask, "How do we know the difference between an ordinary dream and one from God?" I have found these two important features in dreams I've had from God. Firstly, there is something very unusual about the dream. For instance, one summer when I was of college age, I spent my mornings babysitting a young lad. When school started in the fall, however,

I could no longer continue taking care of him. Then one night several months after I had last babysat him, I had a terrible dream. In the dream, as I was taking care of him, he ran out into the street. Consequently, I spanked him, and, to my horror, he died. I remembered the dream very clearly when I woke up the next morning, and to my surprise his mother called and asked me to babysit him that very evening. However, when I told her about the dream I had had, she decided against my staying with the child. I have no idea what might have actually happened had I babysat that evening, but one thing I do know is that something bad was going to happen, and I avoided the bad situation by heeding the warning of my dream.

Secondly, the person remembers the dream clearly the next morning after waking. We do much dreaming during the night, and most of our dreams are never remembered. But dreams from God are still uppermost in our minds when we awaken.

There are several other means by which God warns us: people through whom God is speaking; a gnawing feeling that something isn't right; and by circumstances. However, regardless of how we are warned, heeding the warning is of supreme importance. But even if the dream or warning is never actualized, it never hurts to change our plans.

CHAPTER 11

THE ROAD MOST
TRAVELED

One of our favorite European countries was France. We liked the people, their cuisine, and the beautiful scenery of the country. Consequently, we went over there almost every weekend. Since we lived only ten miles from the border, my mom liked to take rambling back roads that twisted and turned and went through many small villages. She said it reminded her of her childhood.

But one time we took a road that wasn't so pleasant. It was my Christmas vacation in 1970, and we had taken a southern route through France on our way to Barcelona, Spain. When we got to Frejus, France, the wind was blowing so hard that I could barely keep the car on the highway. We later found out that this wind was the tail end of a terrible tornado a little farther up in the Rhone River valley from where we were traveling. We decided, rather than going on any farther that day, to stay in a small pension-type hotel for the night. Our room was very cold. The storm had knocked out the town's electricity, and so this hotel had to generate its own. The generator was located in the room next to ours, and its continual starting up and shutting off kept us from sleeping. And because of lack of sleep and the coldness of the room, I came down with a bad sore throat and cold.

As we started out the next morning, we ran into rain that eventually turned into snow as we went farther on. The big-flaked snow kept coming at us so hard it looked like a snow curtain. I could hardly see to drive, and whenever another car passed us, their tires would pick up buckets of snow and smash it into our windshield, and for a moment I was not able to see at all! The snow got heavier and heavier, and the highway got slick with ice as nightfall came on. This did not look like the sunny French Riviera at all. Snow was everywhere. There was no sky or ground anymore—just snow! We were only able to go about five miles an hour, as this was some of the slickest ice on which I've ever driven. I wasn't even sure we could make it to a town where we could find lodging. But we finally did make it to a little town called Beziers and found a cute hotel right on the town's square.

Since the next morning was clear, we decided to try and go on—which was a big mistake. We could only inch along on the ice. At the next town, Narbonne, we got into such a traffic bottleneck that it took us forty-five minutes to go only a few blocks. And all of the town's supply of tire chains and snow tires had already been sold out. Because of this, I decided to head back; but once we got back to Beziers, the sun was shining, and the snow was melting. So we decided maybe we could make it on to Spain, and we turned and headed back toward Narbonne. This was our second mistake! Again we got caught in the bottleneck at Narbonne. By this time the cars were lined up almost back to Beziers.

We saw many wrecks. There were cars wrecked all along the highway. In fact, there were so many that we stopped counting them. We also stopped counting the ambulances going to the wrecks. And there was blood on the snow along the highway where wrecks had occurred. The French were just not used to snow and ice like this, and as one newspaper put it, "They drive like race car drivers." They just did not know how to drive under these unfamiliar conditions. One paper said ten thousand motorists were trapped in this part of France and over six hundred people had been injured.

As we sat in this bottleneck waiting, we noticed that about every other car that did get through from the Spain side had either a bumper or a side dented in. We've never seen such a mess in our lives. I finally noticed a British car got through, and so I went to talk with the driver. He told me, "Forget about going on. It looks like a battlefield down the line." He went on to say that it had taken him all day to come only forty miles. We decided, right then and there, if we could get our little "Bug" turned around, we were going to try and head for home (home being my apartment in Pordenone, Italy). And we did get back safe and sound without even a dent or a scratch on our little car. We saw both French and Italian cars stalled along the way, and some were completely buried in the snow, but our little German Volkswagen just sailed right along.

On another trip to France we had problems, but this time the problem was fog rather than snow. My mom and I had started out on Thanksgiving Day headed for Rouen in the Normandy area. But as we got closer to Rheims we found ourselves engulfed in dense fog for miles on end. I could hardly even see the pavement as we headed north. We finally decided to turn around and go back to Rheims. We praised the Lord for leading us almost blindly to a fine hotel—Novotel, a chain of nice hotels in France and around the world—where we stayed overnight.

Down in the hotel restaurant we ate our Thanksgiving dinner, consisting of a salad of cold salmon and various greens, escalloped veal (very tender and nutty tasting with cheese and bread crumbs), a huge baked potato, and a serving of baked leeks. For dessert we had, instead of our traditional pumpkin pie, pear soup! This was a liquid pear sauce with tiny bits of chocolate floating in it and a sprig of green mint. We'll never forget this unusual Thanksgiving meal!

We decided the next morning, due to the still-present fog, which was now frozen as ice on the highway, to turn around and head homeward. We figured the ice and fog would only be worse farther north and closer to the sea. Heading back, we soon ran out of fog, and the sun came out as well. When we got to Nancy we stopped at the Daum Crystal Factory, and lo and behold, they were having their semiannual promotional sale. We found several pieces of glass we liked and bought them. So this trip turned out to be profitable after all.

On another trip to France we had had a fun time one Saturday looking around the world-famous glass village of Baccaret, but as we headed for home (home this time being near Karlsruhe, Germany), it began to grow dark. A I turned onto one of the main highways going from Nancy to Strassburg, fog was also developing. Knowing that I had to go through a Vosges Mountain pass in order to get home, I was dreading the four miles of hairpin curves I would have to maneuver before dropping down into the Rhine River valley. Having a difficult time seeing in the darkness and fog, I just crept along. And as I got closer to those hairpin curves, I became so fearful that I was almost hyperventilating. I began to pray earnestly that God would help me.

When we got into the town of Phalsberg, I had several turns to make before leaving town. Somehow in the fog and dark I missed one of the turns, and all-of-a-sudden I saw a road that went straight down into the valley with no curves at all. Taking this road, we were soon down and zipping along on a straight and level highway toward home. Later I went back to look for that road that went straight down into the valley below, and I could never find it. But I'm most thankful I did find it that dark and foggy night when I was so fearful.

From these stories it may seem that all our trips over into France turned out to be adventurous, but most of the time w had no problems at all—rather, we enjoyed a fun and relaxing day.

One of our favorite pastimes was to visit the various glass factories scattered around the country, but particularly found in the Alsace-Lorraine region. My mom had had an antique shop in the Kansas town where she and my dad had lived and, consequently, was knowledgeable about glass, both in Europe and in the United States. So it was a special joy for her to be able to visit these various factories.

A factory that we visited quite frequently was one in a small town called Vallerystahl. On one visit there, as I was going to purchase a vase, the man in charge suddenly grabbed the vase from my hands and began engraving it with the factory name. The engraving was so perfectly done that we assumed he had at one time been their engraver.

Later, as were ready to leave, he invited us, along with a German couple, to visit their museum of glass. This was ordinarily not open to the public except for a few months each year, so we felt very privileged. We followed the manager through their workrooms and up a flight of stairs to a large room where they had thirty thousand pieces of glass. All the glass was covered with heavy dust, and once my mom remarked, "Oh, there's a piece of satin glass!" To which I replied, "That's not satin glass; that's just dust!"

On another visit to this factory, the manager went into a back room and brought out a catalog that showed pictures of early glass made in the factory. And he even allowed us to have copies of several pages from this catalog.

While we enjoyed the glass factories most, there were other kinds of factories that we also visited. Once while rambling through the wine region of France, we chanced upon a gingerbread factory. It was a pleasure just to get a whiff of the wonderful odor emanating from this building, but to be able to munch on some of the products was even more satisfying!

And speaking of food, France is noted for its wonderful cuisine. I'll never forget the savory omelet I had at Le Mont St. Michel, an omelet so light and fluffy—but filling a twelve-inch platter—that I still felt hungry after eating it. Nor will I ever forget the delicious meal, but unusual restaurant, we experienced in Verdun. Upon finding out that our hotel had no restaurant, we asked the desk clerk his recommendation for an enjoyable meal, and he told us to go to the bowling alley! Not knowing what we would encounter, we headed out, following the clerk's directions. To our surprise and delight, we found the area for eating was glassed off from the noisy bowling alley part. In fact, each table was situated in a little cubicle, giving the guests their own private room. And the little room was even carpeted. But the meal of baked sole with potatoes and lettuce salad was exceptional.

On her eightieth birthday, my mom wanted to eat her special-day meal in a little cottage-type restaurant in the Alsace region of France. Having a farm-type décor, this particular restaurant contained small tables with red and white checked tablecloths, wooden floors, ceramic wine jugs on window ledges, and rustic farm equipment on the wall. The meal consisted of a single bowl of boiled mussels, which we quickly downed and then got more. My mom felt quite satisfied when finished that this was, indeed, a special birthday.

One spring, a couple of friends and I were fortunate to get reservations for the world-famous three-star Paul Bocuse Restaurant near Lyon. We each had a delicious three-course meal, but when the dessert cart came around I found I was too full to enjoy the decadent chocolate pastries that looked and smelled so delectable.

I could go on and on about the food in France, but since I have a whole chapter on food and eating, I will now digress to another topic.

Over one Presidents' Day holiday, my mom and I made a spur-of-the-moment decision to drive over to Albertville to see if we could attend any of the Winter Olympic events. We drove from Germany across Switzerland to the Alp Mountain region in southeastern France. We were fortunate to get a room in an almost-new hotel in Chambery, which was not far from Albertville.

We had to park about five miles from the Olympic Village, but buses took people to and from the village. Once there we were able to buy tickets from a lady (probably a scalper) for an outdoor women's speed skating event. The snow was coming down in buckets, and as we sat on the outdoors bleachers our backs were soon covered with six inches of snow. Since the American skater had already lost the race, and we were cold clear down to our fingertips, we decided to leave. Unfortunately, we didn't get to see any of the other events.

Some of our experiences in France were rather sad. Such was the case when we were traveling one summer through the central part of France and came upon a burned-out village called Oradour sur Glane. Every building in the little village had been destroyed by fire. This happened in World War II. Apparently a German Nazi officer had been insulted by someone in the village, so he angrily rounded up everyone (everyone, that is, but one little boy, who, having seen the Nazis in action in eastern France and knowing what they were capable of doing, took off running and hid in a nearby wheat field) and herded them to the village square. The women and children were marched to the little local church, the doors of which were then locked and the church set on fire. The men of the village were lined up in the village square, and each was shot, and the town was then set ablaze. The French have kept the village just as it was left after the fire to remind people of the horrors of war and of hatred. When we were there, a man from Russia was also walking among the ruins. He told us that this same conflagration had happened many times in Russia by the Nazis.

A very inviting region of France was the area known as Normandy. Located in the north, it is an area which is wet and green with rolling hills. Black and white cattle graze all day in lush green pastures with apple and pear trees scattered here and there. Naturally they have lots of cheeses, other dairy products, and fruits and ciders as well as fish. The houses are huge affairs made of stone blocks, many still with thatched roofs, but quite a few with slate roofs and even slate sides.

One very unusual city in this area is that of Le Mont St. Michel. Built on the top and sides of a granite mountain that rises from the ocean, this city has a monastery on its peak and narrow winding streets with shops on both sides. It looks very odd to be driving to the ocean across flat, low, puddly terrain and then to see this mountain sticking up out of the ocean before you. The only way to get over to the city is by a built-up causeway that at times is cut off by the ocean's tides.

Another appealing city in this area is Bayeux, where the famous tapestry (a wool-embroidered scroll) is located. This scroll, which is quite long, depicts the events before and after the Norman conquest of England in 1066.

In the north central part of France we encountered many grim reminders of war. Traveling through this area, we came upon many graveyards of people from both world wars. There were people not only from all over Europe, but from the United

States and Turkey as well. These graveyards were reminders of how horrendous war is.

But no matter how heartbreaking an area was, we always seemed to manage to have some funny experiences. While driving late one night, I began looking for a hotel. Going down one dark street in a small village, I excitedly said to my mom, "There's a camel parked along the curb in a car parking place!" To which my mom replied, "Jane, quit kidding." "Oh yes," I answered, "there really is. I'll turn around and go back so you can see it"

My mom then said, "If there is, it must be a statue." I kept insisting, however, that it was a live camel, but my mom at that point decided I had been driving too long and was just seeing things.

As I slowed down, the car lights shone onto the side parking lot, and sure enough, there was a real camel standing there tied to a nearby tree. Then we noticed in the dim, dark night light a small circus tent across the street!

LESSON NO. 12

THE IMPORTANCE OF MAKING MEMORIES

The difference between really living and just existing is what one does with his or her life. In other words, a person can sit around and do nothing or can grab life by the horns and live life to the fullest. And it doesn't matter what condition a person is in—whether minus legs, arms, or hands, or perhaps crippled or confined to a wheelchair—if one wishes to make a difference in this life, he or she can do so. Some of the people who have done the most in life have sometimes had the least with which to work. It is, therefore, my contention that people really can do what they want to do if they will just get up and start.

Sometimes it takes awhile to reach the goal, and it may be amid many setbacks. But if a person is determined, he or she can accomplish what he or she sets out to do: be it getting a good education; or traveling and seeing the world; or becoming the artist or author he or she wishes to be.

Thus, the important lesson I learned while living and traveling in Europe was to not be afraid to try various projects. For instance, I decided I would like to have college credit from the University of Heidelberg, the second oldest university in the world. Therefore, I enrolled in a course that was taught only in German, and somehow I actually made it through the course!

One of my favorite pastimes was to visit various places in France. This wasn't always easy, as the weather often didn't cooperate. And there were other problems too, such as finding a good hotel for the night or having a problem in understanding the language. But now I have many wonderful memories upon which I can look back.

The important object, then, is to try things and to not give up. Be wise, of course, but don't be afraid of attempting to do something you really want to do. In other words, be daring!

CHAPTER 12

FROM EASTER BACK TO CHRISTMAS

(A letter I wrote to my folks.)

Well, I made it back safe and sound yesterday from Finland. I'll try and give you some of my impressions of the country. I was quite disappointed when we landed, as there was snow all over the ground. There was snow, in fact, from Helsinki clear up into Lappland. I got a hotel reservation made at the airport and then took a bus from the airport into the air terminal in Helsinki. From there I walked to my hotel. It wasn't far, and I had a map, so could find my way with it. My room was supposed to be a moderately priced one, but I had to pay around twenty-eight dollars a night for it. It was clean, comfortable, and warm, though. In fact, it was too warm, and sometimes I'd wake up in the night feeling as if I was in a sauna. I spent Saturday and Sunday looking around Helsinki.

On Monday I got on a train and headed north. I went as far as the train went—to Rovaniemi, a city just a few kilometers from the Arctic Circle. I arrived there about nine at night. It was snowing, and snow was all over the ground. I felt as though I had gone from Easter back to Christmas. I headed toward the lighted area, which seemed to be downtown, and found a real nice hotel, which was again rather expensive. The train ride took eleven hours, as this city is around six hundred miles from Helsinki. About all I saw as we rode along was snow. All the lakes and ponds were frozen and covered with snow.

I found the Finnish language very difficult to understand and found very few people who spoke or understood English. In fact, when I'd ask them in English if they spoke English, they didn't even understand enough to say yes or no.

Most of the restaurants in Finland are self-service. One in which I ate in Rovaniemi, however, had a board with various meals listed on it (in the Finnish language, of course).Since Finnish doesn't correspond to any other language that I know, I had no idea what the meals listed were. I did as the other people did, pushed a button next to the meal wanted, and it actually turned out to be a very tasty meal consisting of a piece of meat something like hamburger that was covered with a mushroom gravy, boiled potatoes, and a salad. Most of the food was very reasonably priced.

The next day after I arrived I left early in the morning to catch a bus that was going up north about two hundred miles to a city called Ivalo. The trains don't go any farther than Rovaniemi, and then the buses take over. The one I took was a postal bus, which picked up and deposited mail along the way. The bus ride took six hours, arriving in Ivalo around two thirty in the afternoon. There wasn't much to see along the way except snow and trees and every so often a farmhouse. Almost all of the houses were built of wood, as they have plenty of trees in Finland. Several times along the way I spotted some reindeer back in the woods. They were a little hard to see, as their fur was the color of snow. We picked up and let off various people along the way. Once, several Lapp women got on the bus. I could tell them by the beautiful red cap that they wore.

Ivalo is a very small town—about two thousand population, I would guess. I walked around town, and after I had seen it all, I headed back to the café where I was to catch the bus back. Imagine my surprise, though, when I discovered that I had earlier misread the bus schedule. Instead of leaving at five thirty (as I had earlier thought), the bus was to leave at midnight! This was quite a shock, as I didn't know where I would go or what I would do for the next six hours. All the stores closed up by 7:00 p.m., including the café at which we were to meet.

I finally decided I would go to the only hotel they had in town and ask if I could sit in their lobby until time to leave. Fortunately, the girl at the front desk spoke English, and she said I could go back to the TV room and wait until time to leave. Quite a few people were back there watching a TV program, *All in the Family* (in English, no less).

At eleven all the TV programs went off the air, and everybody left to go back to their rooms. At that point an elderly gentleman walked into the room. He could speak fluent English, and so he sat down and talked to me. It turned that he was a very prominent man in Finland. In fact, he was one of the planners of a model city outside of Helsinki that is world famous. Prominent people from all over the world come there to see it. As I talked to him, I felt that while he had lived a very interesting life, he had left God out of his life. I just happened to have with me a book of the life of David DuPlessis and had read it about halfway. I felt I should give him that book. So I handed it to him, telling him that I had been reading about a man who had lived nearly as interesting a life as he had, and I thought he'd enjoy reading it. I told him it was in English, and since his English was so good, he wouldn't have any problem reading it.

At midnight the bus came, and we started on our way back. Since everyone curled up in their seats and went to sleep, I did too. Once in the night I was awakened by a noise, and when I looked up I saw the driver shaking snow off the windshield wipers. Then I noticed that the snow was coming down in buckets. I figured that the Finns were used to snow, but even so, I prayed that God would guide the driver and give us a safe journey. Then I felt that since God was taking care of the bus driver, He would want me to go back to sleep. So I did just that.

We got into Rovaniemi around six in the morning. I went to my hotel and slept for an hour. (I had rented my room for that night thinking I would be back in time to use it. As it was, only my luggage got the benefit of the room for the night.) After I awakened, I went back to the train station to catch a nine fifteen train back to Helsinki.

One problem with the Finnish train system was their reservation setup. People can reserve seats, but the seats are never marked as being reserved. So I sat down in a seat by a window, and someone came along and told me that was their seat. Well, this happened to me three times when we first started out from Rovaniemi. And after the third time I was really getting angry. Then I decided to pray and trust God that I could keep the seat that I had. And I didn't have to move anymore.

When we got within two or three hours distance from Helsinki, a Finnish girl got on the train and sat down next to me. It turned out that she could speak fluent English, and we sat and talked, then, all the rest of the way back. As we talked, I found out that she was a born-again Christian. How good God was to give me a new Christian friend! Anyway, she had the next day off, as she had taken a week off between changing jobs (she is a computer analyst), and she offered to show me around Helsinki the next day. So we made arrangements to get together in the afternoon.

I had wanted to do some shopping in the morning and also to get my hair fixed. (My hair was so dirty and stringy, as I had been wearing a tight-fitting wool cap, which really messed up my hair. But everyone in Finland wears slacks, boots, and wool caps when it's cold.) Anna, the Christian girl I met, had recommended a beauty shop in one of their main department stores, so I went there. I don't know if the beautician misunderstood me, or if she just thought my hair needed cutting; anyway, I got a haircut in addition to my wash and set. While I was in the store I did some shopping. It was a good thing I had to meet Anna, though, as I could have stayed there all day and spent every bit of my money. They had some really beautiful things to buy!

Anna and I went in the afternoon to a park where there is a monument built in honor of Jean Sibelus, the man who wrote the song "Finlandia." Then we hopped on a bus and went to Tapiolo, the model city the old man had planned. It is a really beautiful city with modern homes and apartment buildings, and was pretty even with snow all over the ground. In the summertime the grounds are filled with roses, and the ponds have ducks and swans swimming in them. The city is built right down next to the ocean, also. I think the sign telling about the city said thirty thousand people were living there.

The next day, Saturday, I spent getting ready to leave. My plane was to leave at two. All-in-all I really enjoyed my trip to Finland. I found the people to be very nice, helpful, and friendly. And the Finnish women are absolutely beautiful! They are the prettiest women I've ever seen anywhere in the world. It seemed good to get back to the warm weather of Germany, though, as snow can be really tiresome.

Love, Jane

PUTTING ALL ON THE ALTAR

One of the most important decisions we can ever make is that of giving God our all. When we have everything under His control, the devil is far less likely to be able to get us to fall.

This, then, was the important lesson I learned on a train in Finland. Having never been in that country before, I naturally wanted a good window seat on the train where I could look out at the countryside as we took the long trip from the Arctic Circle back down to the capital city of Helsinki. Consequently, I made sure I got to the train station early so I could get that good seat I was so looking forward to.

Finding just the place I wanted, I plopped down, eager to begin the long trip. However, I hadn't sat there long before a lady came and told me that I was in her seat. No problem. I just moved one row back. But I hadn't sat there long before a man came and took that seat. Apparently, these people had reserved these particular window seats in advance of the trip, but since there was nothing indicating the seats were reserved, I naturally assumed one could sit there.

The loss of my seat occurred three times before I gave up and scooted over to the aisle seat. Feeling quite angry, I soon realized that my attitude was evil. And as I prayed for God to forgive me, I also felt that I needed to do something more. That something more meant telling God I would give this whole situation to Him, and if need be, I would even stand if I had to all the way back. But regardless of what happened, I would serve Him and do what was right.

When I gave the whole situation to God, however, something wonderful happened. First, the lady who had just taken my window seat told me that she would be getting off the train shortly, and since no one else had reserved that seat, it would be mine. But second, when the train made its first stop, and I had scooted over to the window seat, a young woman got on board and sat down in the seat I had just vacated. Now this wasn't just any ordinary young person either, for not only could she speak fluent English, but, best of all, she was a born-again Christian. What a wonderful ride this turned out to be! Not only did I have someone with whom I could carry on an interesting conversation, but she also offered to come by my hotel the next day to take me around and show me various interesting sights in Helsinki. How good God is!

But even if God had never worked out anything good for me, the fact remains that nothing should ever matter so much to us that it causes us to sin. When something begins to matter too much, the devil can then use that very thing against us.

This "putting all on the altar" refers to the story of Abraham, who, when asked by God to give up his only son, did that very thing. He laid Isaac, his son, on a homemade altar and then prepared to slay him. But we know from the biblical story that God had placed a lamb in a nearby thicket, thus sparing Isaac's life. However, two thousand years later, Jesus, our Passover lamb, lay down His life for us. God did not spare the life of His only son.

So by "putting all on the altar" as Abraham did, we can live a much more holy life. And when we put everything in God's hands, we can know that He will work out that which is for our best.

The end